MW01230260

ODAR

BOOK THREE

AMIRKANS

Denice Peter
Karamardian

ODAR

other; stranger; foreigner
(in the Armenian language)

AMIRKANS

(pronunciation for 'Americans' by the immigrants of this story, according to elder family members)

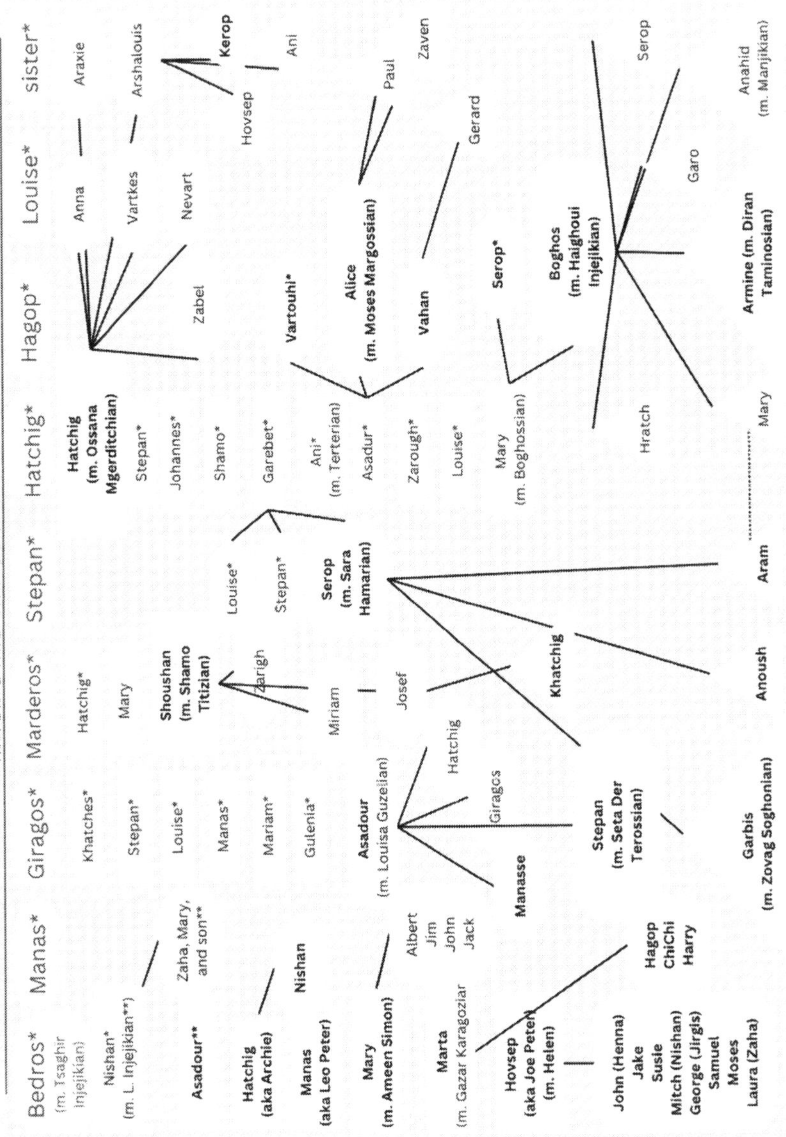

Karamardian family tree approx. 1890 – 1940

*indicates killed or deceased during 1915;

**indicates lost or stolen; names in bold indicates characters in book

Generations Out of Syria

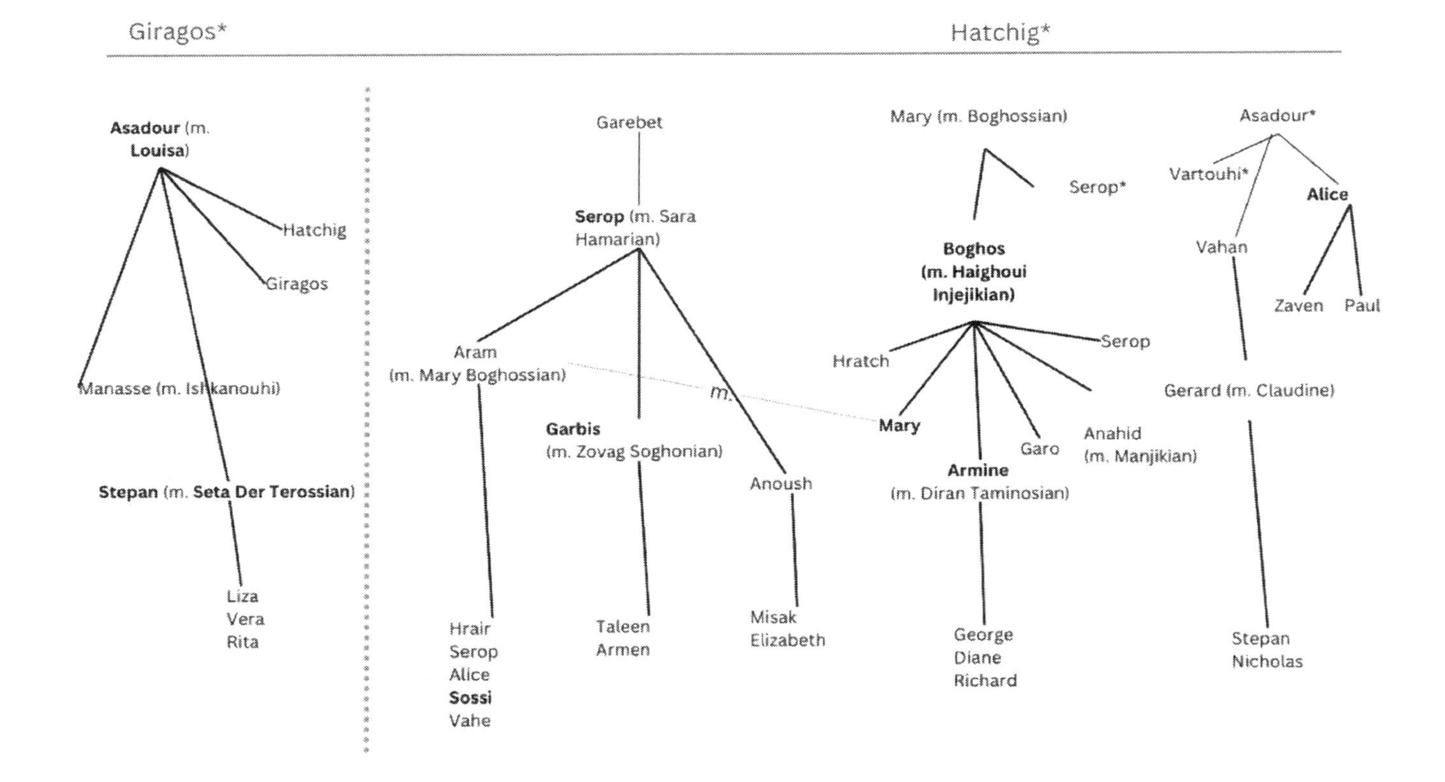

Bedros Line

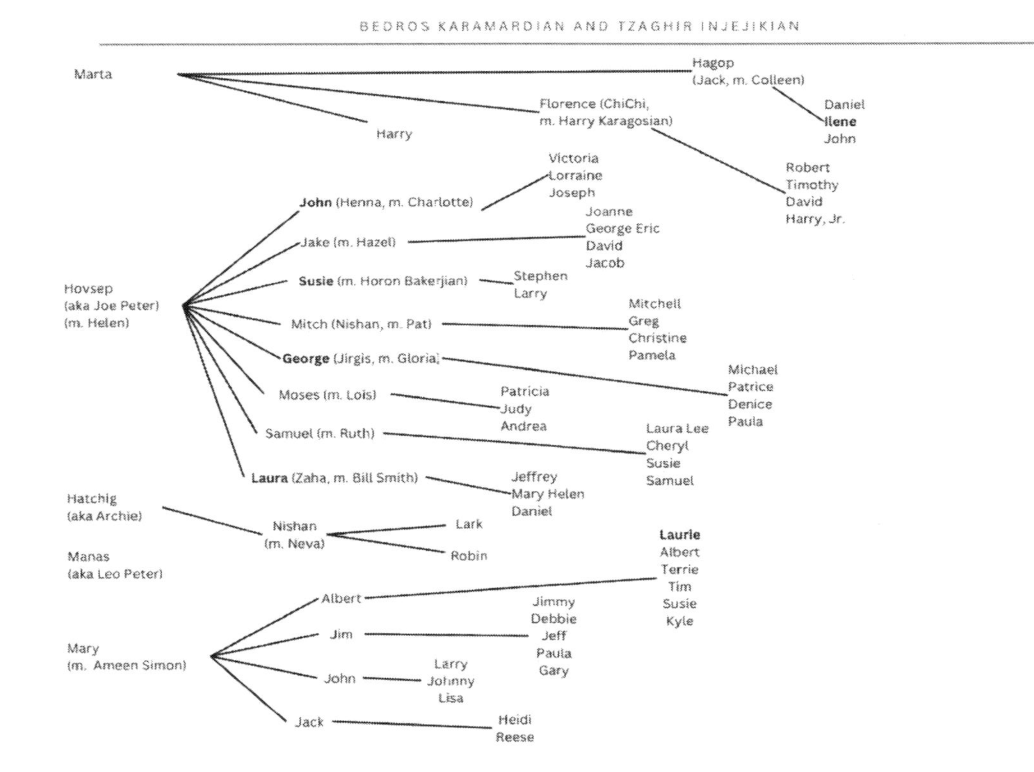

BEDROS KARAMARDIAN AND TZAGHIR INJEJIKIAN
Marta
Hagop
(Jack, m. Colleen)
Daniel
Ilene
John
Florence (ChiChi,
m. Harry Karagosian)
Robert
Timothy
David
Harry, Jr.
Harry
Hovsep
(aka Joe Peter)
(m. Helen)
John (Henna, m. Charlotte)
Victoria
Lorraine
Joseph
Jake (m. Hazel)
Joanne
George Eric
David
Jacob
Susie (m. Horon Bakerjian)
Stephen
Larry
Mitch (Nishan, m. Pat)
Mitchell
Greg
Christine
Pamela
George (Jirgis, m. Gloria)
Michael
Patrice
Denice
Paula
Moses (m. Lois)
Patricia
Judy
Andrea
Samuel (m. Ruth)
Laura Lee
Cheryl
Susie
Samuel
Laura (Zaha, m. Bill Smith)
Jeffrey
Mary Helen
Daniel
Hatchig
(aka Archie)
Nishan
(m. Neva)
Lark
Robin
Manas
(aka Leo Peter)
Mary
(m. Ameen Simon)
Albert
Laurie
Albert
Terrie
Tim
Susie
Kyle
Jim
Jimmy
Debbie
Jeff
Paula
Gary
John
Larry
Johnny
Lisa
Jack
Heidi
Reese

BLACK SEA
RUSSIA
Constantinople
(Istanbul)
Sea of Marmara
ARMENIA
Lake Sevan
Yerevan
TURKEY
Lake Van
Van
Smyrna
Cicilian Armenia
(1080 - 1375AD)
Aintab
(Gaziantep)
Mersina
Adana
Iskenderun (Alexandretta)
Tigris
River
Musa Dagh
Aleppo
Kaladouran
Kessab
Latakia
Der- El-Zor
Jabalah
CYPRUS
SYRIA
Tartous
Homs
Euphrates
River
Junieh
Valley of Christians
Baghdad
Beirut
Damascus
Haifa
N
Tel Aviv
Amman
W
E
Jaffa
Jerusalem
S
Nile
River
Port Said
Rafah
EGYPT
Suez Canal

For family....

Publishing Services provided by Paper Raven Books LLC
Printed in the United States of America
First Printing, 2024

Cover image by Sossi Madzounian
Cover design by Kristin Designs

ISBN 979-8-9900982-5-1

Table of Contents

PROLOGUE

CONNECTION

Ithaca - 1992

AUTHOR

Life changes shape. Barry Lopez reminds us that "You've got to reconsider the organization of the physical world and your place in it in order to find the new orientation you need; if you're not to be done in by the forces all around you." Adaptation is the word that comes to mind when I contemplate my grandfather's quest to create and support his family. (At times, even other families.) I like to, as needed, remind myself of Lopez's words: "This is something that has to be dreamed again." My grandfather reconsidered his dream again and again, ever moving forward for the sake of his growing family. Sadly, within my own life, this ability eluded me for some time: I could have used the tool to save my soul as I approached middle age with some dashed dreams of my own.

I had yet to consider surrendering the career that drove me so hard through my twenties and into my mid-thirties, after which, it became a "set-aside" thing that I assumed I would return to any day. It had felt like a mere detour when I followed my future husband to Brazil and then, reluctantly, to South Florida. Those were his terms for returning to the U.S. and I agreed to the compromise. Meanwhile, a stronger dream was pushing its way into my reality, but relentlessly evading me. My "clock" was ticking at ever-increasing speed. I began a long, slow float through, what I tend to call, my "Dark Ages" and slipped smoothly into an alternative business career, while chasing the more urgent desire for motherhood. Two long, drawn-out attempts at pregnancy, each over a period of three years, were followed by miscarriage.

I had named both of my unborn children in the early months of hope and optimism: Nishan. This was a symbolic choice, in memory of that unknown great uncle who was murdered in his home in front of his family, and whose wife and children disappeared within minutes, into either oblivion or an unknown world of Turkish culture. I was determined to make a 'Nishan.' Looking back, I can't escape the irony of naming the unborn for the "tragic." My own losses were insurmountable, not to be faced, and I was very alone. With no family near, and a husband who was unable to help either of us, I turned to the easiest available coping mechanism—workaholism—to avoid drowning in sorrow and depression. Had I scratched at the slightest surface emotion, a dam would have burst. I was determined not to go there, and so embraced denial as my "go to" tool.

The marriage suffered for this, among other reasons. But the darkness of my days was really rooted in failure: failure to produce, failure to pursue my original dreams, failure even to acknowledge the darkness. Somewhere inside I longed to heal, and this instinct led me home, where such an emotion might safely be allowed to surface. In 1991, I attended a twentieth high school reunion in my hometown after which, desire pulled at me to return to prior dreams and… something else. I began to fantasize a life with summers back in Ithaca; a few months hiatus from work to return to theater projects and enjoy family. So, when I was about to fulfill a financial strategic goal of purchasing a second income property, it made lovely, luscious sense to buy something in my hometown. I envisioned a house or duplex that I could rent to students ten months of the year and occupy for the remaining two months each summer.

The following summer, I set out on my mission with a practical plan to search for an impassionate choice to meet my goals. I chose a realtor named Jane; a no-nonsense, older woman who I came to adore. In those days (I, too, worked in real estate at the time), we carried around printed books of listings called MLS (multiple listing service) books. In Ithaca, the MLS book that Jane handed me was a single, slim volume.

"Here, take this and do a quick look through as a check list on your way home," she told me. I looked at the skinny book in my hand and laughed out loud. In Fort Lauderdale, I explained, I used at least six volumes, all thicker than huge city phone books, and all of which lived in the back seat of my car. (Computers and cell phones were not yet a part of business for most practitioners.)

That day, I had settled on a duplex in a downtown neighborhood called Fall Creek and planned to make an offer on it the following day. But we hadn't thoroughly covered the market and it made sense to drive-by any options that might contend with the initial choice. My parents then lived in the lakeside village north of town called Aurora and, before driving there for dinner, I decided to detour up South Hill to take a nostalgic look at my favorite view of Cayuga Lake from the front of the Coddington Restaurant, an old favorite. As I pulled over at the restaurant, I noticed a sale sign in front of the property next door, a run-down house set way back from the road and on an incline. Had I ever noticed it before? I wasn't sure, but I was pretty certain two sisters I knew from school had lived there, with the surname Capalongo. There is no reasonable explanation I can find, let alone give, for the sudden need that overcame me to get inside that house. It looked like quite a project—faded and peeling forest green cedar shingles, clearly transformed into rental units—and had no curb appeal to me. Yet oddly, it felt necessary to see the inside before I could complete my purchase offer the next day with a clear head. When I got home, I telephoned Jane immediately.

"Jane, do you know the Capalongo house on Coddington Road?"

"Yeeeees," she answered in a drawn-out, unapproving drawl.

"I know it's not what I'm looking for..."

"No, Denice, it's not!" she interrupted me—I could swear like a stern teacher—barely masking her impatience.

"Jane, you have to admit I haven't wasted any of your time, right? Would you just indulge me?"

"But WHY?!"

"I really don't know. I just want to walk through it, then we can draw up that contract."

We met the other agent at the front door landing, above eight concrete steps. From these steps, it was hard to move one's feet away from the sweeping view of the lake sprawling below us. I could almost reach out and touch it. The same was true of the Cornell University campus, in full view on the hill to my right. This all caught my breath, and I only reluctantly turned to enter the house. When we stepped inside the door, face to face with a staircase, I could see where doorways on either side of a long hallway had been boarded over. The chopped-up space was separated in ugly ways, but I immediately pictured some typical bed and breakfast establishments in Key West, one of which I had appraised and my cousin managed, all created from large old conch houses. I envisioned how the now blocked doors to my right and left led into parlors and common living spaces and where the greeter desk would be tucked into the alcove beneath the stairs.

I heard myself say out loud, "What a great lay out for a bed and breakfast!" and was promptly answered with "What a great idea!" by the listing agent.

Wait! I thought, That's MY idea! You can't have it. As soon as the thought entered my head, I sought to banish it. Did I say THAT out loud? I wondered. Then, emphatically to myself, Let that go, Denice! You do NOT want a bed and breakfast.

And as the three of us stepped down the interminable hall I began a silent chant in my head, a mantra with every step: Let it go, let it go, let it go… Until we arrived at a kitchen set at the back of the house.

A square room, as beige as every surface of hallway walls and banister, held only a stove in a corner, a set of white cabinets with formica counter, a hanging—no, dangling—lightbulb, and multiple layers of linoleum flooring. I gave it all a brief glance and shudder, still chanting to myself, as we moved on through the only opening from the kitchen into a dining room space on the other side of the long wall. There, I stopped dead in my tracks.

The dining room we were standing in possessed the only beautiful quality I had found in the house, other than the impressive, panoramic lake view from windows and door—a white ceiling plastered in gorgeous sculptured design. But this is not what brought me to a standstill. It was the scene before my eyes; a hallucination, I presume, but nonetheless as clear as anything I'd ever witnessed. A table, with a low hanging light directly above it, a group of men seated around the table playing cards and smoking cigarettes—among them, my grandfather. My Jido! And they were not speaking Arabic (which I, at least, can recognize the cadence of, along with a few swear words). I naturally presumed din of men's voices was in Italian. But what was my grandfather doing there? The haunting vision was so real I didn't bother to hide it. Whatever I mumbled to the two professional women indulging me must have sounded incoherent. I think I actually backed away. But not before I took in the beautiful swirling design of the plaster ceiling in that dining room, the only special quality, beyond views, of the house.

I raced home that night and burst into my father's office in the library.

"Dad! Would Jido have ever played cards at the Capalongo house on South Hill?"

"I don't think so, honey."

"But think about it!" My mind worked overtime. "He worked at Morse Chain. All the Italians on South Hill worked at Morse Chain. He must have known those guys! It certainly seems possible…."

"No, I think I would know that…."

It didn't matter. I couldn't shake it. I am not one to act impulsively, but what was I to do? I worked the numbers every which way and they didn't make sense. Renting the house, I simply could not break even. But I had made decent money that year and could afford a small loss (if only for that year). Finally, I did not qualify for the asking amount. But I made the offer anyway—what we call in the business, an emotional buy. I told the seller's realtor to beg my forgiveness from the seller, the widow Capalongo, for the insulting offer but I couldn't waste her time as it was all I qualified for. And in the final second I added, "It may not mean anything to her, but just mention that I'm Joe Peter's granddaughter."

I'll never know what knowledge or memories Margaret Capalongo may have held regarding Joe Peter. I visited her the following summer, carrying a tin of store-bought cookies, but she was surrounded by small grandchildren in her kitchen and not in a position to chat. She passed away before I had another opportunity to see her.

The summer following the purchase, my then husband and I spent a month in Ithaca painting the house between tenants. Our elderly neighbor, Anastasia Iacovelli, a member of the Italian families that settled and dominated South Hill, was planting a row of pumpkins at the property edge between our houses. While we chatted, I mentioned that the tax records only reached back to 1921 to account for the property structure, but that I assumed it was older.

"Are you kidding? I was born in the house in 1917! Before that it was the train depot." My mouth was agape, still trying to make the connection as she continued, "Don't you know I am a Centini?" (The Centinis owned the restaurant on the opposite side of my house and, apparently, were part of the same Capalongo family.) I didn't know. And I wanted to ask more about the train depot, but before I managed to formulate that question, from out of nowhere, I heard myself ask, "Nasta (short for Anastasia), did you ever know my grandfather?"

As soon as the words left my mouth, I fully expected and waited for the logical question: *Who is your grandfather?* Instead:

"Joe Peter? Of course! Every Friday night he brought tomatoes for the restaurant and played cards with the men—right in there!" And she pointed through the window to the dining room. Dumbfounded, I could not articulate another word, though I wanted to ask so much.

After my son was born and dreams were dreamt yet again, I moved permanently to Ithaca in search of the right "village" to help me raise him. His arrival was the stuff of miracles, for which I had long given up hope. My marriage limping along to its inevitable end, I needed the best option for parenting alone, plus the best education I could afford, which was NOT to be found in Florida. For two years I worked but, unable to afford after school care, I had no choice but to try to make a living from within the walls of the house itself. My bed and breakfast was launched, along with a private voice teaching studio. These, I supplemented with performance and radio broadcast producing. My aging parents were just twenty-seven miles away, up the east coast of Cayuga Lake in Aurora. Visiting on weekends was important. Life was busy.

The return to Ithaca felt symbolic and weighty, filling me with elation. When I drove up and down the hills that hug Cayuga Lake, I felt as if I had climbed into my mother's lap. The landscape was home; home, the way geography can be inserted into a person's bones and imprint on their DNA like a familiarity that anchors them.

In summers, whichever cousins happened to travel back through Ithaca on any given year would appear on the sprawling lawn that overlooked the lake in Mom and Dad's back yard, the same spot on which my sisters and I held our weddings. Family reunions could be counted on. On the far point of the cliff, Dad had assembled the beloved shish-ka-bob pit, where he held forth with his brothers and nephews, while turning the long skewers of lamb chunks speared between sweet peppers and onions over the grill. For our family, the shish-ka-bob pit and the inevitable clinking of iron hitting iron in a family game of horseshoes had become the modern version of the card tables and shoe shops of Syrian and Armenian male society.

All the Syrian dishes brought by the older generation would lay lovingly on long tables. Some of these were destined for later votes in unofficial competitions—specifically the grapeleaves and kibbeh—of family conversations. Multiple generations fanned out among dock and beach, football games on the front lawn, or shuttling back and forth from the kitchen to the outside tables set up underneath the striped tent that Dad rented every year. Just as when I was a child, I most often found myself hanging around aunts and uncles, reveling in their conversations, straining for more. The uncles had moved to Florida—all but Dad and Jake—but John and Sam, Laura and Susie would typically be present at every reunion.

At one of these reunions, not long after I had moved into the big house on Coddington Road, I walked past Uncle John. His voice trailed me with a question I did not expect.

"Hey, Denice! How's the Capalongo house?"

I stopped in my tracks and turned back to face him—a man as slight as all my uncles, standing spread legged with arms folded under his chest. I had grown up one of twenty-seven grandchildren on my father's side of the family. Children were seldom addressed by an uncle unless it was to say, "Whose kid are you?" I took no offense that I can recall. But now hearing my name from Uncle John was jolting, and his asking about my house confused me. How could he know?

"How did you know I bought the Capalongo house?" I asked, though I immediately figured out he and my father must have chatted about it. Still, knowing whose house it was? I was trying to work it out when I realized that he had already launched into a story.

"Every Monday we stopped at the house and knocked on door. The old lady would come, and Pa would say, 'Where's Vito?' 'Where ya think he is? Go-a get him!' She'd throw her hands in the air and walk away, and Pa and I would walk downstairs to the wine cellar to find Vito lying there. Pa would carry him over his shoulder, and we'd go to work. He and Pa worked up front in the foundry and he would lay Vito down by the stove and let him sleep it off. No one was the wiser." He was clearly enjoying this telling. Then he chuckled, "Sometimes he'd repay the favor and cover for Pa."

Some weeks later, Uncle John visited me and showed me which room in my basement had served as the 'wine cellar.' Thus began a decade of monthly visits to Syracuse for notetaking on John's memories, the same decade during which I flung myself into my middle years—a period of creative projects and businesses, not to mention my son's upbringing. In the background of daily life, my brain thought constantly about the reality of my ancestors and still living family and strained for glimpses of the lives that brought them to where they were at this moment, sharing with me what they recalled and/or cared about.

I found myself driving to the old homestead on the rise of Peter Road, the scene of so many stories. The farmhouse had burned a few years earlier, but I still marvel at the view from the top of that hill, from fields now overgrown and unused to the expanded tree line. The border of jumbled vegetation on the other side of the street almost resembled forest and I'd no idea if this was a current or perpetual state. Suddenly, I wanted to know the answer. To everything. I needed more and realized that there was not enough information. The first generation were all gone now, and half of the second generation as well. Jake and Moosey passed on in that decade. John entered his 90s, Dad his 80s. My mother was increasingly ill, and I felt something crucial slipping away. A new anxiety began to creep in.

I felt settled into my place again. But my confidence, innocence? Neither remained intact. I plunged ahead, busy,

busy, busy. I managed to visit John and Laura as much as possible, even worked out a few trips west to see Susie. Although I told myself there was plenty of time for the story that lurked and teased in the back of my brain, I knew the witnesses were gradually disappearing. And life marched on. There was only, and always, time to dream again.

CHAPTER 1

FARMS

King Road - 1926

JOE

Lent was particularly difficult that year, with so many hungry children in the house rebelling against the forty-day imposed agony of no meat, eggs, or milk. Helen would not relent in spite of Joe's grumbling, "Fasting was not prescribed by Christ!"

But to the kids he said, "Big deal! You couldn't cheat if you wanted to!" This produced a laugh from his eldest son, John, who had grown accustomed to his parents' rigid rules laced with contradictory humor.

The staple of buckwheat pancakes, pilaf and stewed vegetables in tomato, without supplemental protein, had barely stretched and hardly satisfied. So, when it finally arrived, Easter Sunday was the most welcomed day of the year. Joe bought a lamb from a neighbor farmer and, after Mass at the church in Myers, all of Tubbha—the Syrian Hill community—was invited to the farm. The boys dragged sawhorses and table planks from the barn and set up the long tables that filled the yards and were soon covered with unlimited platters of Syrian dishes. Shish-ka-bob roasted on skewers over a pit that Joe, John, and Jake built from loose stones the younger boys had collected. The farmhouse was ringed with rows of scraggly bushes that only redeemed themselves in April, when they exploded into yellow, streaky clusters, like some of the full explosions of fireworks over Cayuga Lake. Joe learned that these bushes were called forsythia, and they became his favorite.

The Abbotts and Mahools came from downtown, and Helen enjoyed a treasured afternoon with her old friends, Alice and Anna. Besides the Syrians from Myers, some of Joe's own family were represented that Easter. In addition to the family of his cousin George Chakalian, Sammy Giragossian, the uncle who hosted Joe in New York City when he arrived in the U.S., now lived just an hour away, in Binghamton, with six boys of his own. Together, the Peter boys, Moses boys, and Giragossian boys made more than enough teams for baseball. The adults tossed horseshoes against the iron rungs permanently pounded into a side yard. To the Finnish neighbors, Easter of 1926 at the crest of South Hill on King Road, looked like a convention of black-haired foreigners, recently immigrated from an exotic place called Syria. But the roaring laughter and smell of roasted lamb would have enticed them to stop by, especially when the occupants waved and motioned to join the festivities—and some did.

When the guests drove away at dusk, Joe caught sight of George, Jake, Nicholas, and Sam as they snuck off to climb the peach trees. He had already warned them not to pick the peaches while still green; it would ruin the crop and make them sick as well. But running the fields with cousins and friends throughout the day, the kids had taken notice of the trees laden with green peaches. Even with full bellies, they could not resist the fruit. Three of them were too little to reach, so Jake plucked and threw peaches down at the younger kids. Giggling, they raced back to the house and headed straight for the cellar door, with the obvious intent to hide in the basement with their stash. The younger boys, Mitch and George, ran—laughing and juggling the fruits cradled in their shirts, without a care in the world—straight into the legs of their father! Joe stood silent and still for one minute. Jake approached from behind, and attempted to slink into the background, to no avail. Joe's anger was a mountain no one could climb, let alone skirt around.

"Every one of you god damned kids get over here!" Every brother and cousin of the household was summoned and lined up for a belt spanking. Even the youngest child of the house was indoctrinated to the consequences of the actions of all—guilty or not. The justice, or injustice, of communal spanking served as their earliest memories and lessons. Joe was consistent with this discipline. He tried to recall his own upbringing. He couldn't summon many memories, other than punishment from uncles, when he was very young and part of a larger group of cousins. They will work it out between them, he thought. That's the way.

The summer farming was easier than usual with the additional hands of five Moses nephews and more of his own now old enough to pitch in. The plentiful vegetables were eaten or jarred and sold. Peaches and berries that year were bountiful; most were taken to market, the remainder canned and preserved by Helen and Mary. Joe baked Syrian bread every single Sunday for the family. He also took his tomatoes to some Italians he worked with at the Morse Chain Company, to their restaurant on Coddington Road. His sons were not old enough to play cards, so playing was limited to occasional Friday nights at the home of his co-workers. This is how he learned about huge swaths of abandoned farmland in the hills of South Danby, though he would insinuate to Helen, without outright lying, that he had heard about it at work.

"Mind you, the soil must be impossible," said his buddy Vito Capalongo. "Why else would a farmer abandon it entirely? They're practically giving it away!"

Joe was intrigued. He went to the county offices downtown to inquire and drove to the South Danby Road on a scouting mission. Almost to its crest, he turned left onto a dirt road and arrived on top of a fairly good-sized hill with soaring views of distant horizons beyond the hills stretching away further south. A handwritten sign identified a farmhouse—a Greek revival classic, with none of the window features that adorn such style homes in town, though Joe wouldn't have known the difference nor cared. All he saw was a very big house. It sat right up by the roadside, and he pushed a creaky door open to inspect. On the ground floor, he found two living rooms, a large kitchen, and four rooms for beds. The second floor offered four more bedrooms plus enough space in the hallway for two more! He could fit the whole clan—hell, maybe three families! A large barn had enough space for a herd of cows. Joe had never been a real farmer; he had so far only managed ten to twenty-five acres of vegetables and fruit groves. He adjusted his eyes to the sun, taking in the 170 acres of overgrown brush and rocky soil, some of it invisible beyond tree lines, and thought 'we'll never go hungry here. I could do this. Hell, I've got a built-in crew!'

Mid-summer, Joe drove to "*Itaka*" in search of the offices of the Salvation Army. There, he discussed the plight of Mary and the kids and secured a promise of help from a sympathetic officer. It could take months, he was told, before suitable housing could be found and established. It was a first step to set up Mary and the kids in a new life of their own. On the second Saturday in August, the grown-ups left John Peter and his cousin Mose Moses in charge of the other kids and climbed into the Maxwell, the baby Moses Peter in Helen's lap. Joe wrapped some of the loaves of his freshly baked bread and carefully set them on the dash. First, they paid a visit to Abraham and Alice Mahool in the west end of Ithaca where Abe cut Joe's hair and the women caught up. From there, they walked over to Abbott Bros store and purchased bulgar wheat for tabouli and kibbeh. Abraham welcomed them warmly and insisted they come by his house on South Geneva Street to see Anna. There, the two men and three women enjoyed tea and Syrian bread. While the women huddled in the kitchen, Joe spoke frankly with Abe Abbott.

"The Salvation Army may come through with a house. We will help, but she will need more income. The boys are still young."

"And the oldest?" asked Abe Abbott.

"Moses. He'll be just twelve in November."

"I can put him to work on weekends and after school for now, until he turns thirteen. But I really encourage that she keep him in school as long as possible. All of them."

"I feel the same. My John is always asking to go to work. I say no for now… fourteen, maybe."

Within the month, a home was found for Mary on nearby Allen Street. Joe helped her and her boys move before the school year began. On Halloween, Mary Moses gave birth to a girl, who she named after the sister-in-law she had depended on. Little Helen was her last child, a final gift from her deceased husband. On January 6th, Joe collected the Moses family to celebrate a final Christmas holiday at the King Road house. Looking around the house as the boys raced and whooped, Joe thought about how small it seemed now, and how limited the crop of potatoes and fruits.

Never mind, he told himself. We'll have plenty of room to spare soon enough. And land to spare, too.

Every Friday thereafter, he drove to downtown Ithaca to visit Mary and the kids. He brought some cash and either canned vegetables, jams and dried fruit, or fresh produce when the seasons allowed. Helen often joined him, unless she was needed at home with a sick child of her own.

The following year, on a clear day in April, the whole family piled into the Maxwell and drove out to assess the new farm. They did not know how soon they could return; as long as heavy snows continued, the road would be impassable. Joe could see that the challenges in winter would pile up; clearly, the dirt-packed road was not suitable for plowing by the county. By the month's end, the snows tapered, and the yellow blooms of forsythia covered South Hill. These especially buoyed his heart when he passed the riotous yellow clumps ringing the Rumsey Farm at Coddington Road on his way to the chain plant. He again lobbied for the night shift so that he could farm by day, and they began the clearing of the land before school let out—on weekends for the bigger kids and weekdays with the littler ones, not yet in school. It was all hands on deck.

Pines and other trees had grown to considerable size since the land had last been worked, so the clearing took all of spring. Joe bought an old Fordson tractor with iron wheels to pull the trees and shrubs out by the roots. On the ground, his sons torched the brush, whooping and hollering at this new game. The tractor often rebelled, refusing to start, which prompted Joe's repetitive cranking to morph into cursing at Henry Ford for making such a beast. On some occasions he resolved the issue by taking the tractor coil into the house to heat on the stove and dry off the moisture. This sometimes worked, but often produced a specific curse in the more poetic Arabic version of "May God burn the religion of Henry Ford, the big one!" Nobody giggled when this was uttered. They seemed to disappear, avoiding the mood that produced it.

In May, once the clearing was well underway, the younger boys ran to explore the house, bounding up to the second floor which would be their domain. Joe chuckled at their backs as they raced by hunting for treasure. In one room, they found hickory nuts covering a floor, left to dry by the previous owner. The tiny nuts had a sweet taste when popped into mouths. While they sampled, Sam looked out the window and spotted the plum orchard some few yards off.

"Will ya look at that!" Joe heard him say, just before Sam and George barreled outside to climb the trees, abandoning hickory nuts for the ripe, juicy Black Nectar plums.

After school let out in June, the family packed up and moved to their new home in South Danby, which sat right on the county border with Willseyville. Two farms flanked them on either side of the long road: one toward the South Danby Road in Ithaca; the other farm belonged to Frank Allen, a Finn with five daughters, whose house was five hundred yards away and whose land extended down a steep, curvy hill shaped liked an "S" to the south. This was called Singer Hill and connected to the main road at Willseyville into the next county. Joe's family would soon discover Singer Hill to be an obstacle course, for both work and play, summer and winter.

Come September, the single-room schoolhouse on King Road was traded in for a similar one-room school on the South Danby Road. Meanwhile, the kids learned to hitch the wagon to an old horse that Joe bought to supplement the tractor, from which they bunched hay. Joe arranged to move the cow from the King Road farm. There was room for serious milk cows at the South Danby farm but first, he needed to work out what crops, besides fruit trees, the rocky soil was suitable for. Summer flew by. The kids explored the land, the woods, and sought out neighbors, all of whom were Finnish. By contrast, the Peter children were the darkest creatures found anywhere for miles. But everyone on the hill were immigrants, trying to eke a living out of inferior farmland that had been abandoned by others, and were somewhat interdependent on one another. By fall, a happy and humming Helen was once again pregnant.

"It's the last time!" she muttered, adding, "And it better be a girl!"

The remainder of 1927 crawled by and they learned how to manage new circumstances. When drifting snow covered the road so that even the horse couldn't pass, they had to drive the horse and buggy through the fields to get anywhere from the farm. Living off the grid in winter, on an impassable road, was a challenge that would regularly need to be overcome, for work, school, and eventually, to deliver milk. But Joe was content with the farm and his family, and when Zaha (Laura) was born the following June, he hoped Helen would now be content. Joe thought again of his first daughter, the first Zaha, of her deep black eyes filled with light, her uncanny articulation. She spoke like a grown woman, whose ancient soul shone through. And he felt her now, whispering into his ear, "There you are, Pa! My gift to you and Ma."

But something was wrong! Helen's afterbirth was followed by blood—too much blood. He reacted like a man still running from Turks: wrapped her up, and the baby, and carried her into the car. He yelled to Susie, "Fix dinner, Susie! And take care of Moosey. John, see to the horses! All you kids, do your chores! Mind your brother."

He drove as fast as he dared. Helen was pale, weaker by the minute. The drive through Danby was too damn long! Down South Hill, then up State Street to county hospital, not quite sure where it was located. Tears were threatening, then pooling behind his eyes, blinding him. He prayed the way he thought Helen might, although it was not his thing.

Once she was handed over to the doctors, Joe found it unthinkable to sit in one of the straight, colorless, vinyl chairs in the room to which he was banished, and where pacing was naturally frowned upon. But when others came to the room to wait, Joe had no choice. He sank low into the chair, into a bottomless depth of helplessness, so excruciating, so very gradually into himself. Fuzzy pictures placed himself somewhere else. He was at home in Ladehkiya on the night Marta was born—the night his mother left him. He and his brothers had fled the sounds, covered their ears, tried to escape the scene. He had tried, in those tiny cracks in the mind, to find his way back to normal life: baking with Mayrig as she told him stories and sang…

Please, Helen, don't leave me!

Eight-year-old Hovsep (Joe) had been paralyzed the night his mother died, a condition he'd managed to avoid ever since. But he felt paralyzed now, hurled backwards through years and continents, while vaguely aware that he must not allow himself this indulgence… with eight children to support. He pushed against a foggy, helpless longing to drown, letting Helen down…

Mercifully, his thoughts were interrupted by the doctor touching his shoulder.

"We have paused the bleeding for now. But she's not out of the woods. Now, do you have someone at home capable of caring for your newborn?" Joe thought of Susie but discarded the thought immediately. She's only ten years old. He numbly shook his head at the doctor, but then, immediately thought of something.

Several hours later, the newborn baby, having been checked all over, was released to his care. There could be no question of the girl's name, no conversation required. Joe tucked tiny Zaha beside him onto the front floorboard, so as not to roll, and turned the car west down State Street hill. At Allen Street, he parked in front of number 114. He knocked on his sister-in-law's door and, when she innocently opened it, "Mary..." Joe, clutching the bundle that was his last-born child, found, at last, the ability to weep openly and fluidly. And no one, but Mary Moses, bore witness.

CHAPTER 2

SCHOOLHOUSE

South Danby - 1928

GEORGE

We did not get to meet our little sister for six whole months. Ma was gone, too. I struggled for so long to wrap my head around any version of Ma besides her strong and healthy self. The week before American Christmas in December, Pa's Maxwell finally pulled up to the house—our house at the crest of our road—carrying three passengers. When Ma got out from her side, carefully cradling sweet baby Zaha in her arms, I almost fainted with relief. We all rushed them in a swoop, clamoring for a peek at the tiny head of thick black hair, while smothering our mother in kisses. But she waved us away, laughing.

"Go on. You'll suffocate us both!"

Since it was winter when Ma came home from the hospital, we were well into our cold weather routines; the ones when adding layers of clothes took up extra time. Throughout the day, anticipation spilled out and over every chore. We each had a rotating turn to milk the cow, that was the first thing. Then we all mucked the grimy, wet waste from the stall, raked new hay from the loft, first letting it sift through the air and settle on the cold cement below to scoop up, and finally, bedded down the cow. All this was done in time for Pa to hitch and load the milk wagon, then drive the team the roundabout way up South Danby Road to the creamery in Willseyville. He had to go that way, since a direct path down Singer Hill was too steep for the horses to safely descend in winter with any cartload. Pa didn't have much of a milk load yet, but he had plans to get more cows and said he needed to establish his place with the creamery, so he always took whatever the cow gave.

Once Pa left, we raced to the kitchen to eat as many pancakes as we had time for, that big brother John cooked, before we walked the one-and-a-half miles to the schoolhouse. When we returned from school in the afternoon to repeat these chores, the new December darkness swallowed us up by the time we finished.

That day, my head was filled up with two things; not only Ma and Zaha's homecoming, but the Christmas pageant was a week away and everyone in school was given solo recitations to perform. While I practiced my assignment on the walk home, I fantasized that Ma would be there waiting to wrap each of us in her arms, as long as Pa would allow such a reunion before chores.

While Ma had been recovering at the county hospital, our Aunt Mary Moses cared for our sister Zaha at her home on Allen Street in Ithaca. Every Friday after work, Pa visited Ma in the hospital and then drove downtown to look in on little Zaha and take food and cash to Aunt Mary and our cousins. We were always impatient for him to get home and tell us how Ma was doing. John fixed some supper on those Friday nights and sometimes he talked about a long-ago sister named Zaha. He wondered if the new Zaha would in any way resemble the one lost. Not only did I hear stories of the first Zaha, but on those Fridays I learned from John that I am the "second" George in our family. Sometimes I dreamed about sibling ghosts named Zaha and Jirgis, who came to "play" with us in our sleep. But I was afraid to ask my brothers if they had this dream, too.

On Ma's first morning home, John proudly showed off for her how he prepared buckwheat pancakes every morning to stuff our bellies.

"See here, Ma, we're stocked up fine: two hundred pounds of sugar, two hundred pounds of rice, two barrels of flour, and ground buckwheat." He and Pa had taken it just that week to the mill to be ground. He'd been doing the cooking and scrubbing, and Susie helped with washing clothes and dishes. Ma had worried for nothing, she said, and she beamed at John. I looked at her face and I longed to bask in her smile, too. I felt proud of my big brother but, right then I decided I would figure out some way to be the receiver of the kind of look that Ma was giving John.

We always celebrated Christmas on the date from the "old country," January 6th, but the church and school events took place on December 24th. The Methodist Church stood catty corner and almost across the street from the schoolhouse on South Danby Road. Any event in the community took place there, and we kids also walked there for church school on Sunday mornings. Ma attended mass at the Syrian church on the occasions when Pa could drive her to Tubbha, at Myers.

But they would come to watch us perform in the Christmas pageant, and we looked forward to the pride on our parents' faces and any utterances of endearment in guttural Arabic that might follow. The best-earned response from Ma was "Ya eineigh in-eck" on the rare occasion when she tenderly addressed one of us that way. It roughly translates to 'You, the apple of my eye.' More often, though, Ma's comments were earthy and abrupt, even laced with profanity.

On Christmas Eve of 1928, the night sky was especially clear and the brisk air bluntly whipped at, but didn't sting, the skin on my cheeks. My brothers and I followed a wide beam of light that poured out from the full moon and lit up a fairylike path. I must have memorized the magic of the night air in my nostrils, the crunch of our boots on hardened snow, and how much I looked forward to the recitations. And my favorite song, "Silent Night," in which we all had a line of our own. When it was brother Sam's turn, he froze in place until I nudged him and hissed, "Boo Ahrrrtha! (That was Ma's nickname for Sam; it meant father of a head because Samuel had a big head and shook it ferociously when he was mad). Speak up, now!" and how the sanctuary erupted in howls at the childish voice of my brother when first it cracked and then—after a big intake of air—Boo Ahrrrtha hollered in a big voice, "Shepherds *quack*—at the sight!"

I laughed, too, but immediately felt ashamed, and terrible for Sam. I guess he learned it wrong, but I know what it feels like. I remembered my first day of school, a whole year ago, when I was just six. I'd been ecstatic to walk with John, Jake, Mitch, and Susie to the schoolhouse on that day. The length of our road was just under a mile to the South Danby Road, and less than another half mile downhill from there was the school, a square clapboard building. Thick woods surrounded it on three sides, perfect for exploration during recess. I skipped all the way, getting ahead of my siblings and doubling back to urge them along. I fantasized that stepping into the room would be just like stepping into a party, or even better, I thought; it would be like entering the books I would soon learn to read. Twenty-two students were divided into eight grades. Each grade went to the front of the room for a session of recitation, while the other grades remained in their seats to study assignments.

The teacher, Olga Allen, was our neighbor, one of Farmer Frank Allen's four daughters. Pa had gotten her the job that year, when the school didn't have a teacher by the beginning of September. I sat at my desk bench, beaming and looking around, only a little aware of some commotion. I was still clueless to the process and hadn't realized when she called the first grade to the blackboard, so John pushed me forward. My excitement for school instantly dissolved to terror on my way to the front of the room. Sounds were coming from her mouth and the mouths of the other students. I didn't know what they could be! I heard Mitch and Jake snicker loudly from the back of the room. I felt my face burn with betrayal. They could have—they should have—warned me! Before that day I had heard one or two words of English, but never like the torrent that was attacking my ears. I bawled all the way home, I'm ashamed to say. And for a whole week, I gave Jake and Mitch the silent treatment.

I recovered gradually, because I was determined to figure it out. But even as I learned English, for many months I was unsure whether the words I chose were Arabic or English and I spit out many mixed-up sentences. John told me he was proud of how well I adapted; he said he had not been so brave when he was six years old. (After another five or six years, when all of us kids were in school, including Moosey and Zaha, we kids started speaking English when we were by ourselves. But we stuck to Arabic at home with our parents.)

After the Christmas break my second year, we kids were sledding at school when I jumped on the back of a toboggan that Ralph Traver steered into a tree. I didn't jump off in time and crumpled into a painful heap. I couldn't walk so the kids had to drag me back on the sled. Olga Allen didn't believe there was anything wrong and ordered me to stand up, but I just couldn't. Someone ran home to get Pa to pick me up. My leg was broken, and I was stuck at home for four whole months because I couldn't walk to school. That took up the whole second half of the school year, so I had to repeat the grade, and that's how I wound up in the same class with Sam.

For those months at home all winter, I liked to sit propped up in the front parlor that Pa and Ma hardly ever used, except for company. I watched out the window for any passing buggy or vehicle, or even an animal. In the dead of winter there was hardly any activity on the unplowed dirt road. The mailman had started to call it Peter Road, probably because we were the biggest family on it. It was peaceful to read or doodle on some paper with my leg stretched on the sofa. That was when I really learned to read and was able to do it without my brothers bothering or teasing me for it, like they would do for the rest of my school life, whenever I took books home. Mostly though, I filled up with warm pleasure when Ma peeked into the room and saw me reading. She would shake her head in an approving way and smile to herself. I began to fantasize that the way I might earn her pride had to do with books and learning. I never brought it up, but I never forgot that thought, either.

One Saturday afternoon, the sun was slanting through the window in that certain way like a curtain parting to let it in; when it bounces off the surrounding whiteness, and little speckles swam inside a stream of light spilling into the room. I gazed out the window daydreaming about something or other when I saw John coming up the street alone: alone, but he pushed a wheelbarrow with some movement inside—a head. It was a baby heifer! All the peace that was wrapped around me like a blanket scattered right then. I couldn't jump up and run out to inspect the load, but I watched all my brothers pour out from the barn and gather around it. As they flocked around the wheelbarrow, it was blocked from my sight.

"Is it alive?"

"Doesn't look too good to me!" I could hear Susie and Mitch through the glass pane.

I was so happy when John wheeled the barrel over to the window for me to see. The poor creature was barely alive, but we kids nursed her into a robust cow—though, I have to admit, she was pretty much healthy by the time I was able to help.

That cow was the start of our herd, which grew to twenty-two! Naturally, our chores expanded. We soon had three or four cows apiece to milk, feed, muck the stall, and bed down with fresh hay morning and night. Afterwards, the cows were driven to graze one of the adjoining fields that were government property and not yet overgrown. Funny, Pa had no use for FDR and the government's resettlement administration program that seemed to have impacted all the farmland on our hill, but he saw no harm in making use of otherwise bare fields going to waste. When the weather improved, afternoon chores were divided up in twos. Whichever pair of us was assigned to graze the herd would groan at the boredom to come, even though hoeing the gardens and haying were physically more tiring. We passed the time lost in fantasies about overseeing the herd on horseback, like real cowpokes!

By spring my leg was healed. One Saturday in May, Ma's bosom buddy from Tubbha, Bahijy, came to visit us from downtown. I was all too ready for the extra excitement in the house. Ma didn't get to see much of her old friend from Syrian Hill. After his delivery rounds, Pa picked up Bahijy, along with her son. Ma took one look at me eyeing the plate of smeed (Syrian farina cake) that Bahijy set down in the kitchen, and sent me packing.

"You walk good now. Go help Mitch with ta hay. Take Teddy wit you!"

Well, Teddy was a bit older than me and wanted to ride with Jake, who was hitching up a brand-new team of horses. The week before, Mitch had been driving the wagon with our old mare Dolly. Wouldn't you know, before they got a wagon length past the barn, old Dolly stopped in her tracks and died where she stood, right there! One second, she was standing, the next, she toppled over, pulling the reins and toppling the wagon as she went down. Mitch managed to jump off, and Pa had to buy the new pair of horses from Doc Miller.

Mitch and I walked out to an open field to bunch the hay that we would pitch onto the wagon that Jake would drive over to us. But this new team got easily spooked and had other ideas. They took off, completely out of Jake's control. Off in the field, we felt the vibration of the hooves and we looked up, just in time to see them bearing down straight at Mitch and me! We barely dodged them. Then Jake directed them towards the tree line to slow them down. When they had almost reached a large maple tree, they split off to either side of it, breaking loose from the wagon that collided with the tree. Poor Teddy was the worse for wear and lost three teeth to that maple tree, and Pa wound up paying the dentist bill. But Pa's fury was directed at the horse trader.

"God damn, Yehn al-abouk!" he cursed the ancestors of Doc Miller. He traded those horses the very next day, even though it was a Sunday!

CHAPTER 3

SUMMER AUNTIES

South Danby Farm - 1932

GEORGE

Late in spring, the sheriff came to our farm. Pa made his Arak whiskey in a copper still. It had lots of arms to it and sometimes it perched on top of the dresser in a downstairs bedroom that was used for guests. Mitch and I were in the kitchen when Pa came running in the back door and hissed at us, "Fast. Grab ta ting and bring it in ta kitchen before I answer door!" We did as we were told, and Pa went to the front door to answer, but just as quick he came running back to us, "Now! Take it to my bedroom. He's comin to da back!" We grabbed up that still and the two of us shuttled it back out of the kitchen, just as the sheriff opened the back door, missing us by a second! He was bound and determined to catch Pa, but he didn't get him. That's when the still got moved to the basement, even though Pa didn't like working down there; even less, having to go outside to the cellar door to get to the whiskey. The sheriff came some more times, but he never did catch Pa making his whiskey or see the still. Prohibition ended anyway.

The whiskey came out for the parties we had in the side yards. Lots of times the Syrians came from Tubbha and also from downtown, like our Moses cousins and the Abbotts and Mahools. The sawhorses were set up, and we dragged planks of wood out of the barn for the long tables. Pa baked bread and Ma made stuffed cusa with squash, zucchini, cabbage, and grapeleaves, adding to all the food the guests brought. Everyone went home with armfuls of produce from our fields and gardens. Sometimes the crowd was made up of Pa's relatives and friends from Binghamton, especially when our aunties came from Detroit. They spoke another language and roasted lamb and vegetables on the long shish-ka-bob metal sticks that Pa kept in a side drawer.

Aunt Martha loved to come the most. Her husband, Gazar, worked on the railroad in Wisconsin and later the Ford auto plant in Highland Park, Michigan. So, Aunty came alone with her three children to spend the whole summer on our farm. She would sigh a lot and say these were her happiest times. At the end of June, Pa would drive to town, pick up things for Ma at Abbotts' store, visit Aunty Mary Moses, and collect Martha and our cousins at the train station. He sometimes bought them new shoes, too. Only one of us would get to ride along, due to limited space in the Maxwell. The second time that it was my turn to tag along, Aunty Martha and family arrived with an extra surprise.

"Hovsep, you left Ladehkiya when she was a baby, so you don't know her," Aunt Martha said, when she stepped from the train with a teensy tiny woman and announced, "Our cousin Alice!"

Alice Karamardian was now called Alice Margossian; she had just arrived in Detroit with her husband and settled next door to Martha and Mary, right on Thompson Avenue in Highland Park. I listened carefully when they explained all this to Pa, who seemed anxious to talk but he didn't. When the car pulled up to our big farmhouse, cousin Hagop—we call him Jack—leapt out to hug Mitch and Sam, knocking them both down. He is bigger than any of us, and older than me and Sam. Second is Florence; we call her Chi Chi and she follows us boys around because Susie typically ignores her. Harry, the youngest, was pals with Moosey. Predictably, they raced off together to the barn. Later in the day, I lingered on the porch where the grown-ups were gathered to sip iced tea and Pa's homemade Arak whiskey from the still. Everybody else was down picking fruit in the orchard. I was surprised to hear Pa start a conversation. That's not like him. And he spoke in Arabic, out of respect for Ma, I guess, instead of the "auntie" language. I was too curious to run off just yet.

"Were you taken, Alice?" He looked nervous to ask this, and immediately hesitated. But Aunt Alice took no offense. She seemed extremely practical and good-natured.

"Yes, but they put me on a train to the orphanage. They tried to make us Turks, but I memorized my name and remembered it. When the war ended, priests came. They gave us back our names and took us away to another place."

"Did they return you to Kasab?"

"No. Well, you see, I wrote to Asadour. Katchig sent for me, but I asked to remain at that school and complete my studies. What life would I have in Kessab? I needed education to work. My parents… all gone." Everyone on the porch got silent. Aunty Martha nodded and Pa looked at her tenderly. I wondered what he was thinking about, but then Aunt Alice talked some more.

"After the second orphanage, I went to Antioch for university. I almost finished, in 1923, I think—but… Kamal came to power. They were sending the Armenians to Greece to escape him, so I returned to Kessab. I was a teacher. At the Evangelical school."

"You lived with Asadour?"

"No, with cousin Khatchig. He has lots of daughters and one more girl in that house was no problem." She laughed now—a deep, resonant laugh. "Asadour and Louisa are dear to all. Karadouran will miss them."

"Why? What happened?" Pa stiffened, looked alarmed.

"Oh, Hovsep-jan, Asadour gave up the shoe shop, moved to Ladehkiya…. after the boys..." she stopped for a moment. Pa looked real puzzled. She looked at him and said, "Hovsep-jan, they lost their two oldest sons. Typhoid. They still have a little one, Manas. Asadour works now for the French government, I think, from his connections from the war…"

I looked at my Pa as he pressed his temples. I wished I could see what he was thinking. His head shot up when Aunt Martha made a noise like a sob. Something triggered her, I thought. Everyone seems sad. Then Alice said something that puzzled me.

"Have you no word from other Asadour… your brother?"

My Pa looked down at the ground when he shook his head. I barely heard him say… in English, surprisingly, "Sout America is far. After war… how he find us? No one left back dere!"

"Chi Chi, Susie! Don't follow those boys up the trees!" Ma broke the spell, and the mystery. Suddenly activity buzzed once more. Usually, after supper, the yard filled with sounds of broken horseshoes hitting the iron stakes in games of pitch. But Jake was an avid ballplayer, a very good one, and at any opportunity, he would spearhead cousins and brothers into teams in the side yard. The adults watched from the porch rockers. Dusk descended and they remained rooted to the moment, rocking gently, and sipping the warm red Arak liquid mixed in the cold tea. We listened to the yells of my brothers drunk on adrenaline, punctuated by the cracks of wood hurtling balls through the shadowy sky. The sky deepened to the point at which even a white baseball could no longer be followed by our eyes, making it even more exciting, and I finally headed to the yard to join in. But not before I heard Pa, again reach somewhere for English words, maybe to show off to Alice:

"Aha. Here is game I not know in ta old country. Amirkans tink tey invented the fire shows in sky—but, we knew tem back tere. But tis baseball…"

Often, our other Aunt Martha, the one from nearby Geneva—she was Ma's cousin from Syria—came to the farm, too, with her three kids. Aunt Mary brought her four boys a couple of summers from Detroit, and so did Uncle Archie, all the way from California, with three more! We had so many cousins in summertime that the hallways upstairs were lined with beds, just like the bedrooms. It was one big dormitory on the second floor; the adults all slept downstairs in the guest bedrooms, the girl cousins, too. We took all the cousins to swim at Allen Pond at the foot of Singer Hill, while the aunts collected berries from bushes that outlined the edges of our fields. There were usually fresh berries with breakfast for the whole houseful, and the aunts would swoon.

What made those summers really fun were the gadgets that we constructed for games. We boys played cops and cowpokes in the enormous barn; it offered ample space for hiding. Twelve-inch-square hand-hewn beams provided the setting for chase scenes and the weapons we built were brilliant. We all participated in the design and construction of wooden pistols and rifles, even leather holsters to hold them. But the real genius was in the bullets. We sliced inner tubes about a half inch wide, then stretched the rubber over the end of a barrel and back to fit under a trigger that was held taut by another stretched rubber beneath the barrel. The rubber bullets ricocheted around the high loft spaces, sometimes bouncing against wood framing and landing in muck, while a dozen or so of us dark-haired

Middle Eastern boys swaggered like Mexican cowpokes along the barn beams, twenty feet high above the ground!

Pa occasionally picked up some cheap used buggies and surreys at auction for us to strip down to four wheels, and breach between the axles. This made for a fast and light vehicle to steer down the treacherously steep Singer Hill. The hill was cut into layers of rock and at many places rode like a set of steps. During winters we rode the hill on homemade sleds, but on the buggies, we never made it to the bottom without tipping over. In the rare case that someone did reach the foot of Singer Hill, he would end up in the pond.

Level ground could be just as much fun, and so too, the sloping yard that descended to the hen house with its tapered roof. The game was to build up enough speed downhill and get as close to the hen house as possible before steering away. Our boy cousins from Michigan had already had turns one day when Sam and I coaxed Chi Chi into taking a ride. We pushed as fast as we could and when the buggy neared the hen house we gave it our all. It ran straight into the hen house and Chi Chi landed on the roof, hens squawking up a ruckus that brought Ma running. Chi Chi was shaken, but unhurt. Still, not a single boy on the farm escaped Pa's belt that day.

The summer Aunt Alice came, the sawhorses and planks came out of the barn to be set up for another party—this time for the Armenians from Binghamton. Some of them were related to Aunt Alice, Pa, and Aunt Martha. The Giragossians came, of course. We saw them every summer and they had six boys, like us. One of them was good pals with John. Their ma was a cousin of Pa's, though I don't know how that works, except Pa stayed with them when he got to this country and when they lived down in New York City. They came this time with some Kakusians, and many more friends who also came recently from their hometown, Kessab. We kids got confused at times when a cluster of visitors would lapse into the Kessab language that in no way resembled the Arabic we knew. Most of them, I guess for Ma's sake, spoke in the Syrian they had also learned in the old country. When the cars pulled up to the yard, men, women, and children piled out, handing over platters of desserts and salads and hot kufta, that Ma called Armenian kibbee. Aunties Martha and Alice held central court, embracing friends who they said they had not seen in over a decade, and whom, Alice told my Pa, she had not seen since before her "abduction." There were games and races going on everywhere, but I couldn't help myself from lingering near these less familiar adults; they told amazing stories that seemed unreal.

Then, I saw Pa taken aback—astonished, actually—to greet a man he had known in childhood. The man had only recently arrived in the United States. Overhearing the two men mention Kessab, I crept closer to hear more. My Pa never spoke of the old country, and Ma's stories were confined to her own village. Somehow, I knew that catching Pa's words would be something special. The men smoked their cigarettes and squatted under a shade maple, while the meal was being laid on the tables. They discussed a mission school and various classmates who had emigrated.

"And what of Hagop Minassian?" Pa asked nonchalantly. "He taught me to smoke. We were seven," he chuckled. Then, "Did he go to Sout Amirka?"

Suddenly, his old friend was sobbing. A grown man! Shocked, I inched closer, leaned in behind the tree, unnoticed. The man cried a few minutes before he spoke again. Pa seemed frozen, watching him.

"It was awful! I was running from the Turkish army. In desert… I saw our friend buried in the sand—only his head sticking above, beaten by the sun. Ants were crawling into his eyes." He stopped for a moment, choked, and then made a sound like the dying possum Jake speared last Thursday in the barn. I realized I was holding my breath while I wondered if the man had been saved. It felt like a long time before Pa's friend spoke again.

"I could not stop to help him or the Turks would have caught up to me. I would have suffered the same fate as Hagop!" and then he wailed again.

I tried my best to lay still all that night, afraid to sleep, my eyes wide open. I was grateful for Jake's snoring, which usually drove me berserk. If I allowed my eyes to close I saw only sand and ants swarming all over a human head, like moving dots, and… the look on my father's face, a look I'd never seen… I couldn't tell what it meant—how he felt. Helpless? The visions were beyond my comprehension. I battled them for days, trying to focus on good things around me: I counted the herd, appraised the amount of fresh straw available, counted the cousins at the table, counted meals we ate together, and days they had left to stay with us. But there was a cloud in my brain that I wanted to understand. Gradually, it occurred to me that my aunts from Detroit City had survived certain secret horrors, too, but whatever these were, could not be discussed or inquired about. I remembered snips of things mentioned in passing by Ma— never Pa—and now, I wondered. The very next summer I accidentally eavesdropped on another conversation among the aunties.

Aunt Mary and her four boys came that year. Again, we had a Christmas of cousins on the farm, though the Simon cousins were more tentative and unused to farm living. My older brothers enjoyed playing tricks on them and watching them squirm, which made me feel sorry. But they were teenagers, and I supposed they could take care of themselves. As usual, a dozen boys were spread out to sleep on the second floor. The three girls slept in a downstairs bedroom, with Susie in charge of four-year-old Zaha and, reluctantly, eight-year-old Chi Chi. Most of the household was asleep one night, when I needed to relieve myself. I stumbled down the staircase heading for the back porch, surprised that the creaking of the oak planks on the stairwell didn't seem to wake a soul. But the aunties and Ma were outside, talking very low in the rocking chairs.

I stopped abruptly inside the door, just as I heard Aunt Martha say, "I cannot sit on my porch for long. A Turk lives on my street. He walks past every day."

"Marta, get ahold of yourself. You have nothing to fear in this country." Aunt Mary sounded impatient, but Aunt Martha began to cry.

"Oh, my nieces, those poor children, where could they be?" she wailed now. Ma reached over to touch her hand and Aunt Mary said to Ma, like she wanted to explain.

"Nishan's children were stolen by the Turks. The Red Cross couldn't find them. They are either dead, or fully Turks, not remembering…" Aunt Mary seemed to rest her thoughts, but then she sighed and said more.

"Alice tells us many of the lost children forgot who they are, even some who were at her orphanage. They gave them Muslim names and made them become Turkish in every way." I crept backward, back through the kitchen and out the front door to pee. Back in bed, I wondered who were the "stolen children." Finally, full of mysteries, my eyelids sank and closed.

CHAPTER 4

DEPRESSION

Peter Road, South Danby - 1933

GEORGE

When John finished the eighth grade at the schoolhouse, he went to work with a road crew for a couple of years. Then he got hired at Morse Chain and went to work with Pa every day. He was real proud to leave afternoons with Pa for the night shift. We had a snowy winter that year and played outside with toboggans we made and anything else we could rig together. Zaha was now five years old and took to crying at being left behind. I wanted to take her out to make snow people and do kid games with her and told her so one day.

Ma yelled at me, "She doesn't have the proper clothing to fall deep in that snow! Leave her be!"

The sound of her wailing haunted me, but it haunted John even more when he overheard Ma. His first week at work ended on a snowy November Friday and he took his paycheck downtown on Saturday to the department stores in Ithaca. He got home pretty late that night. He'd had to walk all the way to and from the Danby bus stop. This time it was Ma who burst into sobs—of joy or pride, we couldn't tell—when John unfolded the brown paper to reveal a child's snowsuit. It was snow white in color and it was for Zaha. That winter flew by pretty fast and was filled with Zaha's joyful squeals and a snow figure or three.

The summer of cousins and Peter antics also went rather fast. On a particularly hot evening, after all relatives had left for home, our whole family was spread outside to capture any small breeze that might swirl its way onto the hilltop. The adults rocked on the porch and the boys gathered into formation around the makeshift baseball diamond. Susie, a teen, leaned on the porch railing fanning herself. Ma, also fanning, stopped and shaded her eyes, fixing her gaze on a figure trudging up the road.

"Now who could that be?" she murmured to herself at first, then called out to the field, "Jake! You know all the bums from here to eternity. Who is that drunk coming down the road?" Jake, who regularly absorbed the worst of assumptions, was sincerely offended.

"How do I know? I've never seen him before!" he retorted back and resumed the wind up to an interrupted pitch. But we were now all fixated on the mirage coming up the road.

Within minutes the person was upon us. When the dust that his feet had kicked into a light cloud swirling about him began to settle back to stillness, he staggered forward and revealed himself to be an old, quite raggedly dressed and dirty man. The pack he heaved off his hunched back was filled with needles, threads, and things that clanged together inside and

I sensed or imagined my Pa's heart lurch in empathy for the peddler; according to Ma, he himself had begun life on this side of the world that way, when still a young man. Imagine a peddler way out here in the middle of nowhere, probably all of us were thinking. Ma's voice cut through everyone's thoughts. She asked the man in her broken English if he had eaten supper. He said no but begged off any charity. Ma was not having it.

"It seems to me that you haven't had any food in some time. Susie! Go fix a plate of food for the man!"

"We can't feed every Tom, Dick, and Harry that comes by!" retorted Susie. "Besides, I already threw out the leftovers."

"Don't give me that! Fix him some eggs and bread, then! Go on. Git!" My mother was furious with Susie's attitude.

The man remained silent while the grown-ups waited, and we kids shuffled our feet on the field. Nobody talked; we all assumed that the man did not speak our language, but it was clear that he had not eaten in a while. When Suzy returned with a plate, Pa poured him a cup of Armenian anise-flavored rye whiskey, a bottle he kept on hand for special occasions, and again fell silent and watched him eat. I surrendered to my curiosity and wandered closer to the porch just as the man finished his meal and handed the empty plate to my sullen sister. And then, he spoke!

"Thank you. I come from the same town you come from," he was looking directly at Ma.

But it was Pa who asked, "What do you mean? Are you from Ithaca?"

"No. I am from Syria." He was still speaking English.

Ma erupted, her hands a flutter. "How dare you! How could you let us insult you like that and not tell us you speak Arabic!" She continued to yell at him, as if to deflect from absolute horror at herself. Nobody on the porch that night missed the irony, but the man laughed.

My parents insisted he sleep the night, again to the objections of Susie, who muttered to Ma that the man might be a thief or a murderer. Ma waved her off and made up a nice bed for the man. The house could have been filled with three sleeping families, but as far as our family was concerned, there was always room for one more. In the morning, Pa drove him the twelve miles to the Ithaca station and gave him five dollars. To my knowledge, no one asked where he was headed.

On the following Sunday, our parents returned home in the late afternoon from visiting a newly married couple. We stopped our game of horseshoes, entered the house, and asked Ma if she had a good time.

"Yes, but that poor man," she answered.

"What's the matter?" John asked her.

"She didn't even invite us to a cup of coffee," Ma used an actor's lamenting voice, like she did for storytelling.

"What are you talking about?" Pa was exasperated. "I heard her ask you three times to stay to dinner!"

"Three times? That's not enough!" Ma clucked her tongue and lifted her chin. We looked at one another in a way that indicated we'd better pay attention to this rule.

However, our attention was diverted immediately. It seemed the outing had produced something else, too. Somewhere between the farm and the visit, Pa had picked up a battery-operated Zenith console radio and brought it home. Sam ran out to the barn to get the generator, while the rest of us chatted and buzzed and stroked our hands over the wood of the console. The battery for the radio was a car battery, and we charged it up with the generator, that was connected to a windmill. Pa and Mitch had mounted the windmill onto the roof earlier in the summer, capturing the ample wind supply on top of the South Danby hill. Already, a cord and single lightbulb was strung to the kitchen in anticipation of a power source, and the battery was all that had been needed. Now the battery could supply both the lightbulb and the radio. As of that winter, a new entertainment entered our farmstead. The place by the stove where Ma had held court for years with her storytelling was now taken over by the old radio. Ma's stories of Melkia were still enjoyed occasionally: she'd slip them into our lives at various times and places. But her place as our daily entertainer was supplanted with fireside chats and radio plays on bleak, chilly winter nights. And we improved on the battery system over time, creating even more electricity around the farmhouse.

By now, my older brothers were regular pinochle players—John, Jake, and Mitch. At times they let Sam, Moosey, and me join in. Saturday night games were family time and absent of any serious money exchange. But Pa's friendships at work had grown, and his Friday nights spent with the Italians' increased in regularity. I paid attention to Ma on the weekends because she often was upset. John told me there were times Pa left Vito's poker table not sure how he made it back home to South Danby, like sometimes happened on trips Pa and John made to visit the Binghamton relatives, taking turns driving but neither of them sober enough. Saturday mornings brought a tension in the household that caused everyone to find chores in the barn or outside to avoid stumbling into the path of Ma's tongue lashing. Since Friday was payday anyway, Saturday morning always began with Ma counting money.

Uneducated though she was, she was uncanny with numbers and always, always knew exactly how much Pa had lost on a Friday night—or won, though this happened less often, and was never rewarded with a smile or nod of approval. When the clink of coins could be heard on the table in the kitchen, everyone bolted. Pa's rounds to individual egg and milk recipients were wisely scheduled for Saturday mornings and he casually avoided the house until mid-afternoon, by which time Ma usually had settled into a smoother mood and, having tired of her righteous anger, made a conscious effort to hold her tongue from further abuse.

There was a morning, though, that I entered the barn for chores and was stopped short at the loft ladder by the sound of a soft snort. I listened for a moment, hoping to identify the animal making the sound, but then I realized it sounded more like a snore. Curious, I climbed the ladder and found my father curled in the hay sleeping. For another moment I stood looking down at a man who was obviously too proud to let his wife know how badly he was feeling or that he was in need of sleep, and a light feeling of tenderness fluttered through my body. Pa worked hard and appeared to have indulged hard as well. But Ma is right, I thought. He should not be pitied. And I tiptoed away, deciding to ask John about it, but nobody else.

"They musta busted out the wine," said John when I brought it up. "Vito told us he makes eleven fifty-gallon barrels of wine a year—ten red, one white. Pa doesn't suffer from drinking his own Arak. But the wine is brutal on all of them. We'll pick up Vito on Monday afternoon on the way to work and find him sleeping in the wine cellar. Pa will carry him to work, lay him by the furnace and cover for him all day. Sometimes Vito covers for Pa. Somehow they manage to get enough steel out and not get caught." The image of my Pa inebriated and helpless didn't square with my fantasy of him: capable enough to do anything, grow anything, invent anything necessary to make us comfortable. Vulnerability was not present in our family life, at least in my experience of it up until now, and considering it made me… uneasy.

I knew Pa worked with his friend, Vito, in the foundry and also the pickling room, cleaning steel. John started at Morse Chain as a heat treater, carburizing raw steel, packing the steel into twenty feet long, fourteen inch diameter rods, and heating. He was really proud about working with Pa and I couldn't blame him. We all looked up to Pa and our oldest brother, and dreamed of working when we were through with school. But I also felt sorry for John that he only finished the eighth grade.

I really liked school. In June, just before summer vacation, the teacher asked me to stay and talk to her after the school day ended. I was pretty darn scared. I couldn't imagine what

I might have done wrong. So, you coulda knocked me over with a feather when she said, "George, have you considered registering for the college track when you enter high school?"

I honestly could not think of a response. The truth is, I had dreamed of college a lot but tried to push the thought away. It was out of the question: I knew Ma and Pa didn't have money for it. Plus, I had gotten quite used to hiding my interest in studies from my brothers, who mercilessly teased me whenever I brought home books. Emotions about my future easily got mixed up and overwhelmed if I allowed them to linger, which I might have, had there not been enough chores to occupy my attention every single day of my life. Complicating things even more were the words I heard Pa say to Ma a few weeks ago. The English translation seemed something like: "Damnit! I pay taxes in that county too, so I want the boys to attend the good school. At Itaka. I can change to day shift and drive them in. So I told that man!"

I really don't know how Pa made out, but he was adamant that we go to Ithaca schools instead of Spencer. It seems the farm is just over the border from South Danby where our schoolhouse was. We technically lived in Willseyville, another school district, and Pa had a fight on his hands. I was not sure why he felt so strong about it, and I had little doubt that Pa could win any fight he took on, but I couldn't know for sure where I'd be going to school next year. Meanwhile, the South Danby school was finishing up in a week. I did not know where to place the conversation with the teacher inside my head. So I decided to freeze it, for now, and ran to catch up with my brothers.

Sam, Moosey, Mitch, and I had decided to hurry with our chores and play some ball afterwards. Once we rounded the corner from South Danby Road, we started racing each other up Peter Road. I was feeling the weightlessness of late June and a new summer stretched out ahead of me. But almost to the crest of the hill, we suddenly saw Pa speed past us! He didn't even slow down or wave, like he would have on his way to work, but left us in a cloud of dust, gawking after the car. A queasy gnawing began in my gut and was moving upward to my chest by the time we reached the house. Susie was just standing by the road, looking a bit dazed.

It was Ma. Again! I thought my legs would give out underneath me while my sister filled us in and then went to look for Zaha, who would be waking from a nap. Susie had left the schoolhouse way ahead of us, since she was expected home promptly to help Ma. I knew my big sister liked school, a lot. She confided in me sometimes, on the walk to and from, about the hours spent inside with the teacher, who complimented her for her ideas and reading abilities. She talked of how these were the moments of her solace, in contrast to responsibilities at home, where she got singled out and never in good ways. Zaha was only five and Susie, fifteen, was the only available girl. She was expected to match Ma's relentless energy and productivity.

That afternoon, after she got home and cleaned the kitchen, she told us she stole away for a moment, to read in the front of the house under the maple tree. Ma had come out and bent down to pull some weeds along the roadside. Susie looked up and quickly turned back to her book, calculating the number of minutes she might have remaining before Ma snapped at her to be doing something useful and to put the book away. But no words came. Instead, Ma had straightened up her torso just as a horse and buggy drove up along the road, from the direction of the Allens', and Susie heard the soft clucking to the horse that brought the buggy to a stop in front of our mother. She looked up once more, this time at Miss Jennings from down on Willseyville Road, stepping down from the buggy. She seemed to be motioning to Susie.

"Yoohoo, come here!" Susie ran up alongside our mother and saw that Miss Jennings was peering at Ma and said urgently to her, "Is your husband home? Tell him to take you to the doctor."

Then she looked at Susie and said much more forcefully, "No. Tell him to come out here. Quickly! Take her to the hospital!"

CHAPTER 5

DAUGHTER

South Danby - 1933

SUSIE

I was aware of the late spring air while I sat under the tree reading. Or, I should call it early summer, when the lilacs are still lingering and wildflowers already popped up along the roadside ditches. Under that tree, I felt like I was at the top of a mountain. Actually, that's not far-fetched, since our farm sits on the topmost spot on the hill. Peter Road rests here, then runs downhill and, in just a few yards, crosses out of our county into Tioga. Mostly, I was feeling that electric buzz when school ends. For me, it meant moving on from our little schoolhouse to a new beginning in fall, at the big high school. All of this was interrupted when Miss Jennings brought her buggy to an abrupt halt and called out.

"Get your father, now! Tell him to take her to the hospital!"

When I turned my eyes from Miss Jennings to Ma, I realized that Ma's face was ashen, and for a minute, I froze, rooted in my spot. Then I found my feet and ran to the barn, yelling all the way for Pa. Damn it! How could Ma not tell us she was doing poorly? How did she not know? Since I was four or five, when any of us kids tired of working, Ma would snap, "Tired? I don't know that word. You're too young to be tired!"

Now I thought, How ridiculous it is that she ignores her own condition. How can we look out for one another? Should I have been able to see it myself? My head spun round and round, with thoughts tumbling out of it.

As soon as Pa peeled out from the gravel, Ma's head leaning back in the front seat, I kicked the grass and a clump of it flew up in the air. You'd think with all the kids in our house… well, maybe we need a doctor on the farm. I thought about last summer when the boys went down to Allen's Pond and Sam yelled, "Last one in's a rotten egg!" Then he promptly dove in and split his head open. Moosey and Laura ran all the way back up the hill, but Ma and Pa weren't home. What if John hadn't been home? John has his own car now, a 1929 Model A Ford, and he rushed Sam to the hospital in it. But first he packed his head in a towel and that's what saved his life. Someday, someone's going to die in this house. You'd know that just by looking at my brothers. Not a single one of 'em is without permanent scars somewhere on their bodies. Not all from accidents, either; hell, half the marks are from horsin' around.

Like George: he was only three, damn it, when the older ones played cowboys and chose George to be the cow they needed to brand. I don't think a one of 'em told Pa or Ma, or we would have all gotten the belt, even little George. The breeze on my face felt soft and cool; it beat back the heat off the top of our hill for a good part of summer, but it did nothing to alleviate the gnawing worry I had in my stomach. Ma is getting sick too damn much, I thought, and went inside to see what could be done for supper.

Turned out, Ma had to have an operation. It was a modern thing, where they take out the uterus, but only half of it. Partial Hysterectomy. I memorized the words and continued thinking about it. When I went with Pa to visit Ma at County Hospital, I watched the nurses the whole time, in and out of the room, up and down the halls, at the station at the end of the hall. Boy, I sure would rather have that life than living and working on a farm, I thought. The other thing I thought about was this: I may be fifteen, but when I get married I'm not having any ten babies and counting. All Ma's health troubles must come from being pregnant every single year since she got married young, half the time still nursing.

I thought I had it all figured out for myself and couldn't wait for school to start. I envisioned myself marching right into the high school that Jake attends, with a brand-new confidence to maintain high marks. So I could become a nurse.

But as soon as Ma's surgery was over, and she was resting back in her hospital room, reality came crashing down at home. I'm not sure why, but I imagined that life would be a little easier for me during that time without Ma on my back all day long, barking orders to do this thing and that thing, wash, iron, clean, take care of Zaha (who was only five). Most of the household chores were due to having so many brothers. Man, they make a lot of clothes to deal with! And besides that, I had my own barn chores—the worst one, too! Somehow I usually got stuck with hitching the shit wagon and dumping the contents down at the tree line, while my brothers busy themselves with haying, milking, and hoeing. None of them had my double duty—inside and out.

My favorite time was Saturday mornings, because Pa sometimes took me with him on his rounds to the Italians. Though he never said so, I knew he was doing me a favor, thinking to get me out from under Ma's thumb. And later on Saturday afternoons, while the boys tinkered with beat up carts or cars or fake guns, or whatever the heck they were into that day, I walked down to Hilda's house on the farm at the end of the road. Everyone for miles, from South Danby to Spencer, were from Finland, with a few Swedes thrown in. Not only were we not Finnish, our black hair and dark skin stuck out like the midnight sky in a blonde world. Even though Hilda was a Finn, she was the only girl at school who gave me the time of day. Lots of times, she preferred to make an excuse to come to our place instead. That's because she was sweet on my brother John, and I'm pretty sure he was sweet on her, too. But nothing was gonna come of that, I could assure anyone. He cannot marry her. John really listens to Ma, and Ma is adamant about one thing. She constantly says some version of it: "Marry a foreigner and you'll die of a foreign ailment." Meaning, marry outside your clan, and you'll die from a new disease. John did have a couple of Finnish friends like Charlie Olsen and that Jones boy. The three of them were always together before John started working at Morse Chain this year. Which brought me back to my dilemma.

When Zaha was born, and Ma stayed in the hospital for half a year, I was only ten that time. John did the cooking and

Pa did more baking than usual to keep our bellies full. Now with Ma gone again, and John and Pa both working, everything was left to me. Jake, a senior at Spencer school, played ball with the county team and was never at home, and the rest of the brothers raced between school and chores. And so, I couldn't even go to school! I had to work all day long: besides my usual chores, I had to do Ma's work and the cooking. It was so unfair. I lost a month of school already. The only part I didn't mind was getting Zaha ready and sending her off to kindergarten with Mitch, George, Sam, and Moosey. Lucky her. I'd always wanted a doll and Zaha was the next best thing, except when she got stubborn with that little mind of hers. Still, I didn't have much time to spend looking after her or making up games for her, so she just followed the boys around.

This was how my dream faded. When Ma got home she needed to rest for some more weeks. Finally, she landed back on her feet just when it was the beginning of September—and my entry into high school! I had just about finished my eighth grade when it was cut short in June, but I figured that wouldn't keep me from going into the ninth grade at Spencer school with Jake. I brushed out my clothes carefully and pictured seeing Hilda's face when she saw me that day at the big school building, which I'd only seen from the outside when my brothers and I went to watch Jake play ball.

But when I got ready for school Ma asked where I thought I was going and I said, "To school, of course!" I didn't think I was sassing or disrespectful, but she slapped me. I kept my sobs to myself all day and when Pa came in from the fields to get ready for work, I ran straight to him, crying that Ma wouldn't let me go to school. I don't know why I thought he would defend me; maybe he showed solidarity with Ma as a basic rule. Then I thought that maybe Ma was jealous, because she didn't get to go to school. She couldn't really believe it when she claimed girls don't need school! And I knew Pa's sister Aunt Martha got full school, and other relatives, too, so why not me?

But Pa didn't come to my rescue! The worst part was, nobody in this family of mine cared, or seemed to notice the injustice of it or my unhappiness. My brothers were delirious in their daily discoveries and oblivious to mine. Don't get me wrong—it was not like anyone had it easy on our farm, except maybe little Laura, our 'darling' Zaha. But she didn't know the difference anyway and was just starting school herself. I walked out the back porch to the berry bushes that lined the first field and kicked every rock I encountered from the barn to the bush line, noticing that even the blackberry bushes showed just too little fruit to bother with. I sank to the ground and sobbed until the crying was too exhausting to go on, so I closed my eyes to daydream. I thought about the first few years at the little schoolhouse that my younger siblings still walked to every day. I pictured that year Pa got Olga Allen the job teaching (he went to the Association and told them to hire her), and she tried so hard not to play favorites that she made fun of anyone who misbehaved.

One Friday she cried and huffed—I can't remember why—and on Saturday, she sent her father over to tell Pa, "She's sorry but your boys have been naughty again and she's not going to take it."

"Well," Pa said, "Let me find out who is wrong—you or them," which really surprised me since Pa is the type to whip everyone first and never bother to ask which one is the culprit. I didn't hear his conversations with Jake, Mitch, or George, but I tagged along behind him when finally, he marched over to the Allens and told them, "I can't order any punishment because she is the wrong one."

There was a big controversy, and the school was gonna be without a teacher until she finally agreed to stay, because she needed the job. That's when I began to imagine Pa has more of an open mind than I ever thought. So, I got really confused. Why couldn't he see his way to valuing education for his daughter? This was the twentieth century and he always seemed impressed and amazed by things that represent "progress." But when my siblings marched off daily to fill their heads with learning, I remained stuck at home—the servant.

Actually, after a few months, Pa took me to the new pocketbook factory near Pa and John's plant and they gave me a job. Though it wasn't school, at least this was better than being at home, subject to Ma's constant expectations, and I could understand the value of an extra salary more than adding two pair of hands to housework. Maybe it was his way to make the best of it for me, since Ma would not relent. And I got to ride with Pa to town each day, at least to South Hill, now that Pa switched to a day shift. It reminded me of many Saturdays, when Pa piled us all in and took us to the park, or for ice cream, or to watch the flames consume a building when there was a big fire. The factory was on a street over from Pa's friend Vito Capalongo, and Vito's daughter worked next to me. The boss was an okay man. He always offered lunch money to the girl who made the most gloves in the morning. One morning when the milk cart came through during break, that girl reached over and grabbed a bunch of gloves I had just fixed. When I reached over to snatch them back, they fell to the floor and got dirty. She reported me and then went home and told her father. But I was surprised and relieved that Vito actually stuck up for me that time. Pa never mentioned it. And she didn't bother me again, either. I just kept my nose down and told myself, one day I'll get out of here and become a nurse.

CHAPTER 6

City Aunts

Detroit - 1937

Susie

The telegram came the end of June, when school was in the last week and just before the time when Aunt Martha usually shows up with Chi Chi, Jack, and Harry. It came in the afternoon and when I got home from work, the boys had already arrived, read it to Ma, and gone to the barn for milking. When I entered the house, Ma was wringing a rag to death, twisting it up in her hand, and acting like she was mourning.

"That poor, poor girl…" When I asked who she was talking about, she lowered her voice like telling a secret and said Aunt Martha was in the hospital.

"Is she having woman problems, like you did?" I asked. Ma stopped her hand motions and stared at me for a minute. Her face turned stormy, like I had said something offensive.

"It's terrible. Much worse than that. She is taken to a… an institution. She went mad like… we don't know if she will get better…" Ma really was beside herself.

I pictured Aunt Martha in my head, her gentle face. Her smile was a little sad, but it was always there when she was near us kids or talking to us. She never yelled at us like Aunt Mary, who once slapped little Zaha for giving the dog water in a china bowl. Aunt Martha... I stopped still and thought, what does crazy look like? I couldn't imagine. The night was interminable because Pa had left for work before the boys came home and didn't know what news the telegram brought. In the morning, he loaded the milk on the cart and didn't want to talk about it to anyone. We rode to Willseyville in silence, Jake and Pa and I, and on to Ithaca, after he had mumbled something about "we'll talk about it on Saturday, as a family." I guess he meant the only time we were all at the house at the same time, but I wondered why the family had to discuss this all together. What did it have to do with us, other than whether the cousins were coming this summer?

If only time could go back a week and not arrive on Saturday. Ma fixed a mid-day meal for after chores, when normally we would all be dispersing in many directions for afternoon play and stuff. Everyone ate. Then she talked. Martha is sick, she started.

Then the bombshell: "Susie, you will take the train to Detroit on Monday. You'll help out the family while Martha stays in hospital...." I felt my world go dark and still, not exactly sure what it meant.

"But, Ma! Why me? I am contributing a salary to the family!" I was wailing, screeching. I didn't care.... I noticed a couple of my brothers look at me with pity, and I hated them for their freedom. Nobody was sending them to Detroit. My world was collapsing, and I wanted to—was ready to—race out the door and run away, but Pa...

"Enough!" he roared. Oh God, when Pa raised his voice there was no hope for it. "Family is family!" And that was his last word.

Can a sixteen-year-old be more bitter than me? I thought this repeatedly as the train clambered through Ohio. I wept a few times, but I couldn't stand the looks that other passengers shot toward me—either pity or contempt, I could never tell and frankly, I didn't care. My self-pity consumed me—and set me up for misery, too. I wish I knew then what I learned later in my life. I could have saved myself so much anguish. But I was destined to spend my teen years as a household servant to others. Against my will.

I couldn't blame Aunt Martha. Yet I did. And Ma and Pa. And even Uncle Gazar; he was so kind I sort of resented him for it, since it did me no good in my despair. But I especially seethed with rage at Chi Chi, sometimes even Jack and Harry, my cousins. None of them said so, but I was to be their maid. When Uncle Gazar collected me from the station and took me to the house on Thompson Avenue, Chi Chi, only eleven, greeted me like she didn't even know me. In fact, her eyes glazed over most of the time when she spoke. I suppose she was afraid for her mother and too young to be proactive or to understand my role, and I tried to think well of her. Yet she was the first to ask something of me—help with her clothes that needed mending or weren't ironed properly—and seemed not to even know how to fix her own food, let alone help me in the kitchen.

I found myself cooking from breakfast until supper, since it was summertime and the kids were home all day.

The boys seemed disappointed to miss out on their summer break on our farm and weren't used to being in the city when school was out of session. They ran in and out all day to play, acting lost and ready to chase after anything. Even little Harry spent lots of time on the street watching older boys play ball and other block games. As I watched him, I thought of little Zaha back home, the same age. I gasped, recalling the morning that Jake, Mitch, and I got the bright idea to put Moosey and Laura in the bucket and haul them down the well to see how the sounds would carry up to us. John came by and scolded us, reminding us how every child within a mile would suffer the belt whupping from Pa if he got wind of it. So we cranked the babies back up and told them to keep this game a secret. Sighing, I admitted now to myself that I was homesick.

The work for me was non-stop. There was a boarder, too, who also had the name Harry. He worked days with Uncle Gazar at the auto factory and then joined us for dinner. The only relaxing part of each day was when, after supper, Uncle Gazar would lean back in his chair, bring out his pocketknife, peel pieces of fruit, and pass them around the table. We dutifully nibbled on our plum or apple slice while he, without fail, repeated his dessert mantra: "Fruit is so important for the digestion."

Did I mention that Aunt Mary lived upstairs? Uncle Gazar and Uncle Ameen had bought the two-family house together about three years earlier. The Simons had four boarders on their floor. The wooden staircase between floors had no buffer and echoed through the building when boys and men thumped up and down the stairs, making a racket that reverberated inside my own head. Aunt Mary's boys were older than Aunt Martha's: Albert was nineteen and working, John was my age, Jimmy fourteen, and Jack just twelve. Mary's Jack (Jacob) would play with Martha's Jack (Hagob) but the other boys did their own thing. This should be none of my business, except for the booming of that staircase on the other side of the kitchen wall; it thundered with the constant feet of males who know only how to run. After only three weeks getting used to my household responsibilities, Aunt Mary appeared in the kitchen one afternoon and said, "Susie, when you finish cleaning that sink, will you please come up to help me?"

What she meant was: my house is next. And not just to "help" her. I arrived on her floor and was put to work! First, after she had prepped an evening meal of stuffed cusa and put it to simmer on the stove, I was to clean the kitchen spotless. Then she had me dust and mop the living areas—all while I still had a meal to finish for Martha's family and boarder. I was furious. If I thought I could telegraph my parents and tell them to send me train fare, I would race straight out on the street to do that, but, of course, they would not rescue me. The work doubled: Mary expected a chunk of my time every day. Not only did I feel like I couldn't keep up and was in a constant state of panic, I had read the Cinderella story when I was seven. I knew what hell I was living in. It seemed like the longest year of my life.

CHAPTER 7

CITY OF LOSS

Latakia, Syria - 1939

LOUISA

Our part of Ladehkiya was once a glorious district; this, the missionaries often tell me. Our little stone hut squats behind an old church, both grown dreary from the centuries that have worn away at the stone's luster; it's as if the glory days of the Crusaders for whom the walls were built chose to strip away residual life, packing it up and taking it with them as they receded into history. The only traces left are the regular echoes of Yemeni shoes on stone, stones that remained crumbling and forlorn. Yet the persistent sounds of the city are comforting. The multiple number of languages in the city seems to increase every day. The cacophony of foreign tones has always buoyed me, as I hurry through the streets to the mission. I sense the safety in the presence of foreigners and diverse cultures, shielding us from the whims of ruling Muslims, just as we had been saved by British and French during the slaughter of the war, only decades ago.

When Asadour packed up the shoe shop in Kessab, the last thing he did was to remove the sign from the door that read, in Kessabtsi, "Gone hunting." That handwritten sign reflected the carefree joy of our early lives together, before our boys, Giragos and Khachadur, were lost to us. Perhaps, our life in Kaladouran had been too good to be true; for a while, the simple village life among our people had represented a small, but comforting triumph risen from the ashes of our parents, siblings, and ancestors. The very fact of our survival was enough to sustain us. Losing children, however, was too much a burden to ask of anyone expected to continue life as before. Accepting employment from the French army was Asadour's way to heal through change. When he told me, I heard the resignation of a man ready to both acknowledge a certain regret and also to put it behind him.

"Louisa, Amirka is not an option for us. A job with the French is." He did not need to voice the silent words in his head: it is time to give up on waiting for U.S. immigration to reopen—and the French owe us. Indeed, he had earned any advantage the French army had finally to offer. Asadour and the others had risked their lives for the false promises made at wartime.

Contentment gradually found us here, in new city life and in the education of the children that now graced our lives. The mission school is the blessing that connects our past with our future through our children. Manasse was born within weeks of our move to the city. It seemed a blessed omen. I held my breath for more than two years but, thank the Lord in heaven, he did not contract the illness that had taken the others. Then—as if a reward for troubles, our steadfastness, our adaptation—along came Stepan in 1933. We'd been through a lot, Asadour and I. We were granted two gifts in exchange for our sorrows: two boys for two boys. I thought—oh, how foolish of me—that the pain and suffering were finally behind. Now, however, I have much more to endure—alone.

The life we re-created was to last little more than a decade before Asadour's lungs took him from us. All too soon we were thrust into a time not unlike the years during which I and my siblings survived in the Hama camp. This new Ladehkiya life—now, of survival—at first felt cramped and sullen. Nor did Asadour's work with the French shield us from the instant poverty that was delivered in his absence. Perhaps, it is well that we no longer were able to remain in our home. Without him, it might have been unbearable. I was now caught in a deja vu of life: losing Asadour and relying on missionaries to stay alive had happened once before. This time, however, Asadour would not reappear, striding into a dusty Hama camp to collect me and begin a new life.

Still, angels appear in many forms. When we were evicted from the house the French had provided, the missionaries saved us and provided our current lodging. In return I help at the mission, providing all sorts of service, as needed. Recently, I found work as a seamstress in a large store that sells everything a soul might desire, let alone need. The people there are so good to be with. In the afternoons, my Stepan arrives from the mission school. He is allowed to iron for a few hours and earn his coins to purchase his midday meals. He is only a little boy, but loved by the staff and owners and, if teased, makes everyone laugh at his quiet answers.

"Stepan-jan, did you learn the composition of frogs today?"

"There are no frogs in Ladehkiya. We can only dissect rats." No matter how truthfully innocent his answer, the room will roar in laughter, as if he had delivered the world's wisest joke in his earnest little voice.

Less than a year later, I am blessed with fresh joy in a new position. Aram DerTerossian, the store's owner, asked me to help his daughter-in-law care for her new infant daughter at the big house. The darling girl matches the grace of her family. The work is so easy, I feel not a little guilt embedded within the blanket of gratitude that cradles my little family. Tending to a baby girl is a glory for which I had given up dreaming. Now it is handed to me like a gift from the heavens. The family DerTerossian treats me, like all their staff, with respect and kindness.

"Have you had morning tea, Louisa-jan?" and "Please, enjoy a rest while Seta is asleep. You need not keep at tasks all day long."

At day's end, Stepan walks to the big house and enjoys several hours of uninterrupted study while I attend to little Seta. We return to our hut just as Manasse arrives from his afternoon job in a restaurant and our little family of three can sup together.

Tiny as it is, our little hut was also a haven through the centuries, huddled behind the skirts of the mother church. Its walls have stood for a thousand years and welcomed pilgrims—crusaders and even apostles before that. Many such huts throughout the quarter, built for overnight stays, filled up with survivors of the marches and massacres of our people after The Great War. These nights I tuck Manasse and Stepan to sleep in the bedroom and sleep myself near the cooking fire in the stone wall. Our outside latrine is tucked along the outer wall and shielded from view by the church garden. We have no electricity in the hut, and ration our kerosene, but I allow Stepan an hour after supper to continue his studies with the lantern.

In spite of the emptiness in a world without Asadour, I am truly grateful for the perception of safety the quarter has granted us. I feel the spirits of traveling Christians who passed through before me and slept in these same rooms. I often sense my Asadour here, too, carefully watching over us. Perhaps our first sons are with him, tightly grasping the hands that dangled along either side of his thighs. Among the living and the dead, we are never alone. Here, in the ancient Christian quarter of Ladehkiya, I am learning to cast away self-pity; it will not serve me or my boys. They trust me to protect them, even as they grow strong, self-willed, and capable of so much. The way I know to protect them is the promise I made to Asadour—that their education is not to be sacrificed.

In that promise I have completely failed Manasse, who insisted on working after school. He has always rushed through his classes, anxious to work. I knew well his sense of responsibility would drive him to gradually abandon education. Stepan, on the other hand, embraces his studies and buries himself in books until dusk prohibits his vision. He does well. May God protect him and his potential.

CHAPTER 8

EDUCATION

Ithaca - 1939

SUSIE

Ah, the green fields danced and stretched away from the reflection of my face on the window glass as the train rumbled east again. Once it crossed into southern New York, the monotonous green of flat plains began to rise and swell into low hills that stung my heart with longing. I had no idea how homesick the year had made me: I thought I was too angry at my folks, at everyone! When I saw Pa on the Ithaca Lehigh platform, I ran and flung myself into his arms. He seemed slightly surprised but laughed anyway, and the drive home to South Danby was my favorite ever. While he drove, Pa even listened to me when I described my days, but he didn't say anything except to ask about Aunt Martha.

She had come home. I stayed on another few weeks while she rested. She liked me to hold her hand sometimes and still seemed rather sad. But eventually she began to get up and even started cooking. I assured Pa she was better, and he seemed relieved. I asked Pa what was wrong with her and didn't really expect him to answer, but after a minute he said, "Marta saw too much. She can't get over it."

I wished I knew more. I wished I could have helped her. I thought of the day I had asked Aunt Mary about her, and immediately regretted it. As soon as I realized that I had entered into an unspoken world, I thought Mary might hit me or something, and braced myself for the reaction. But Aunt Mary got real quiet and said only,

"She was too young!" I looked over at her, her lips now squeezed tightly and she banged the pot she had just washed when she went to put it in the cupboard—not like her at all. It made me wonder, what did Mary see herself?

The answer will never be spoken, so there was no point. I knew only one thing: Martha fears and hates Turks sort of like the way Ma talks about Muslims that raided her village at night, stealing away the donkeys and horses that they brought back in the daylight and demanded payment for. When Martha came home from the hospital, she liked to sit on her front porch every afternoon around four with tea. But without fail, a Turkish boy in the neighborhood who everyone knew—Ollie Maskike—walked past the house on his way home from school; when he came near, Aunt Martha would turn and go inside. She said she couldn't bear to look at his face, which made me feel kind of sad. Man, he was just a kid!

And Chi Chi was just a kid too, I told myself in my last weeks there. Much as I resented her—or maybe envied—for her innocent life of school and the kindness of gentle parents, even I could see she was confused and frightened by her mother. When I sliced up some watermelon for a snack one afternoon, Chi Chi hissed at me, "My mother doesn't allow any watermelon rinds. Cut off the rinds and throw them out, quick!" I gaped at her in disbelief. Then she looked around—maybe remembered that her mother wasn't home—and whispered, "She says when she was a slave, she only got the watermelon rinds to eat from the woman." Everyone was in turmoil and seemed to take it out on me, except maybe my uncle. Even young Harry spent more and more time in his room where he practiced blowing into musical instruments.

Now that I was home my resentment dulled a bit. But my problem hadn't faded. I wanted school in the worst way. I re-entered the house cautiously, with some trepidation. I was still mad as hell at Ma and she knew it. We acted cordially for about a month. I resumed my housemaid status for a time and watched Ma fawn over little Zaha, even when she brought a book home from school! (Ma had slapped a book out of my hand once.) George, Mitch, and Sam were attending the high school in Ithaca, which surprised me. Jake had finished at Spencer, but Pa, it seems, had gone to Ithaca and shamed the school board into letting the other boys attend there. He paid his taxes to Ithaca schools but, as the farm was on the county line and they didn't provide bus transportation this far out, the kids up here were told to attend Spencer. Pa had switched to a day shift so my brothers rode with him to Morse Chain, then walked the rest of the way down South Hill to the high school on Cayuga Street. They waited around for Pa's shift to end, and he would pick them up after. The janitor, seeing them hanging around after school, took pity on them and gave them a little work for some coins; then they could run off to the soda fountain while waiting for Pa.

I was blind with envy. I brought it up again and was dismissed; in Ma's case it can be defined as a decided "tsk!" Pa said not one word! But I got an idea in my head. The next morning I took a big chance. I snuck away after breakfast and walked down Singer Hill to the Willseyville Road and looked for Miss Jenning's house, taking a chance that she might be home at that time of day. I had a sneaking suspicion that Miss Jennings, a spinster, might be a nurse. At the very least, she was the only person I could think of to ask for guidance. I was rewarded! She was not exactly a nurse, she said, but she was at home and she did talk to me at length. I took the chance, maybe my only one, and said my dream out loud to her.

"You will need to finish high school first, there's no getting round that," she said, which made anything else a moot point, so I confided in her, spilling my troubles like a sieve.

"Well, you may have to leave home to accomplish your goals. Are you prepared for that?"

"I'm already seventeen." I nodded. I should be finishing next year but I hadn't begun the ninth grade.

"I will look and ask around and come visit you when I have any information that may be helpful to you," said Laura Jennings. I think she told me she was in social work, though I did not know what that meant.

True to her word, Miss Jennings came back around up the hill a couple of weeks later in her buggy with the single horse pulling it. Ma offered her tea and forced her to sit and eat something. There's no denying Ma her hospitality. Miss Jennings had saved Ma's life that time, so Ma was respectful and listened quietly while she told me what she came to say. Ma's eyes bugged open wide but she didn't speak, for which I was visibly relieved. Later, when Pa and the boys came home, Ma still remained closed lipped when I explained to Pa and anyone else who cared to listen, what plan Miss Jennings had brought me. I was so shocked when no objections flew back at me that I just sat there stunned—along with Pa and Ma—who acted like they were equally stunned. I wondered what they were thinking, why they weren't fighting me on my plan. Did they feel ashamed? Nah, I doubted it. I would wonder some more but, for now, I put the mystery aside and got busy getting myself ready to move and start a new life.

I was shaking by the time I knocked. Pa drove me and seemed genuinely sorry to see me go. He didn't say much on the drive but at least he asked a few questions like, what grade would I be in. Ma said practically nothing when I left the house, only a grunt as she pushed a basket of berries and peaches into my hands, a gift, I suppose, for my employer—she didn't explain. Now, at 817 East State Street, I was at a door and realized I was trembling with excitement. The large house sat back from the road with two floors and ornate trim all over the porch that wrapped around three of its sides. I couldn't tell if the house was fancy or just warm and comfortable, but I loved it immediately. As Pa backed away to the car, a girl younger than me answered the door and politely ushered me in. I don't know why this took me by surprise; why wouldn't the doctor have children?

In fact, Dr. Harry Bull had six children: two boys and two girls at home, and two more older girls were married and living elsewhere. To me the big deal was this: Mrs. Bull was a doctor, too! She was called Doctor Helen Bull and taught at the university. They both loved children and their specialties in the medical profession were called 'pediatrics.' The doctor's office was in the home, with a side door that entered into a medical suite of four rooms: an exam room, an office, a reception room with chairs, and a supply room. My job was to clean the suite every night and to sterilize instruments each morning before my classes. Dr. Bull was the gentlest man I ever met, even more than Uncle Gazar, and his wife was brilliant and on top of everything.

I also did laundry and ironing, but the family had a maid and I was not the "housekeeper." Dr. Bull covered my tuition at Cascadilla School, a private high school on the campus of Cornell University. He also paid me five dollars a week! So room and board, tuition, plus spending money. Honestly, I didn't even care about the dollars: I would live there for anything with that kind and inspiring family. It was clear to me from the start that this family had no need of my services; after all, they had girls coming of age and could afford fancy maids. The two doctors emphasized to me from the start that my first priority was to my studies and that if I were to find myself in difficulty to complete my assigned work, they would prefer to adjust my household duties rather than to compromise my success at school. I knew they meant what they said: their own children all planned to attend Cornell University—even the girls! The sons attended Cascadilla with me and Alice was to enter in the following year. Studying was the job of everyone in this house. I may have been there on charity, but I didn't mind. If it wasn't me, the Bulls would have picked someone else to help.

Each morning after my chores in the doctor's office, Gifford, Christopher, and I had our breakfast and then walked up College Avenue, past the Collegetown shops and cafes where rich college boys—and a few girls—sat with their legs stretched out under tiny bistro tables like they hadn't a care in the world! There was so much buzz and chatter. All the people in that universe were talking about interesting things and laughing at one another's thoughts!

I have gone to heaven, I thought, and will not speak of milking cows again for years to come—maybe never! We picked our way through the sidewalk tables and human legs, turned right just before the bridge, along the gully with a gurgling gorge at the bottom, and, in about one block, would arrive at our school building. After the leaves disappeared from trees in November, we could see across the gully to the engineering quad with young men strolling along crisscross paths. Every morning I turned and sighed before stepping up to the entrance doors with the doctors' two sons on either side of me, feeling like a million bucks!

It was referred to as a small school. The building was compact with two floors, high, rounded windows, and ivy crawling over its red bricks. There was a sunny room for lunchtime with windows for walls on the east side, facing downhill. To me this building seemed enormous, compared to the single room of the South Danby schoolhouse. It was less than a fifth the size of Ithaca High School, downtown where my brothers were attending school, but I felt so lucky to have the focus and attention of my teachers. It was like a family, with only about five students per class. I had a different teacher for every subject; naturally, learning is easy when it fills the whole day. I chose to focus on biology and science because these were crucial to my goals. My favorite teacher, Mr. Doyle, taught chemistry, which I would have to study every year, as well as an introduction to anatomy.

When I returned afternoons, I went straight to Dr. Harry's offices and my cleaning up overlapped with a few patients. I overheard much of the doctor's conversations with his patients and gained a lot through this opportunity. Eventually, the doctor began to ask me questions; at first he inquired about what I was learning, and then later, tutored and quizzed me about my studies as they applied to medicine. Dr. Helen also devoted herself to mentoring her children and included me: she made the most fascinating conversations at the dinner hour and we spent an hour afterwards with coffee and group conversation together. Everyone talked about their day—imagine! I thought of the farmhouse on Peter Road sometimes during these sessions. I could hear my brothers all talking at once, shouting actually, and laughing and contradicting each other. It really was jolly most of the time, unless Pa was mad about something—then everyone made a beehive in all directions to get out of his way. Ma usually laughed at anything the boys did or said, and then started in with her stories about Melkia, her home village. Did I fit in, I wondered now? Though I hated my life on the farm,

I couldn't honestly answer that. I thought of my family with some bit of tenderness now, but I was so happy in my new life I knew for certain that I wouldn't go back.

When the snow started to fly in Ithaca, the temperature dropped quickly. The wind on College Avenue and along the Oak Avenue gorge swirled into gusts that relentlessly attacked the face and hands. Dr. Helen brought me a pair of boots that had belonged to her daughter Mary, and some extra gloves. I saved up $25.00 and walked down State Street Hill on the weekend and bought a new woolen coat at Rothschild's—so much warmer than my old one. I walked all winter long through Collegetown as warm as I could ever care to be, thinking only of my studies. At Christmastime the school shut down for a week. Since Pa and Ma still celebrate the January Christmas on the 6th, I got to spend my first December Christmas in a happy family home with a real fire and caroling and presents... right out of a storybook. Don't get me wrong. I love my family and missed my siblings something awful, but I enjoyed my new digs immensely. And I adored the wool beret I received from the doctors and a scarf Alice knitted for me, all by herself.

On December 26th, Pa came and picked me up. The doctors warmly invited him in when he came to the door, and he looked around, nodding in quiet amazement, and seemed a little out of place. I felt ashamed of the thought as it flew through my mind, and hustled him out by the arm, grasping an overnight bag in my other arm. I had saved up my weekly salary in December and the day before Christmas, I walked downtown with Alice and her brothers. We had a swell time choosing modest gifts at Newberry's and Montgomery Wards, admired the unaffordable perfumes in the aisles at Rothschild's, and ate at Kresge's lunch counter. I bought presents for my younger brothers and Zaha: writing notebooks for George and Mitch, mittens for Sam and Moosey, and a cut out doll for Laura. It was so much fun to see the surprise on their faces as I handed them the gifts wrapped in tissue paper. Ma even smiled and wiped a tear. That was a wonderful Christmas. But classes were to begin after the New Year, so I could not stay until January 6th. After that year, Ma and Pa relented and allowed the family to celebrate on December 25th like all Americans. It sure made life easier once we all began to leave home.

CHAPTER 9

War Again

Buffalo - 1941

Susie

It really galled me that my little brother George graduated a year before me, and Sam the same year as me. In their last years, I started a new habit. I took one afternoon off, each week after school, and walked down State Street Hill to meet them while they were waiting around for Pa to get off work and give them a ride home. I usually did this on Fridays, and two times, in 1940, before George graduated, I climbed into Pa's car with them to spend the weekend on the farm. Ark (our nickname for George) and Sam would go to Andrews Confectionary with the coins they earned from the school janitor after school and I would meet them at the lunch counter for sodas where we enjoyed the leisure time gabbing. It felt exotic; on the farm we never had that kind of luxury, and I would not have paid attention to their dialogue anyway. But now, I soaked up my grown-up brothers' excitement about life, the war in Europe, and the job Ark was going to start on road construction after graduation. Jake, Mitch, and John were all working at Morse Chain with Pa. Moosey chose to start high school at Candor for some reason, and Laura still attended the old South Danby school, of course. So we kids were all kinda split up now, at least during the day.

There was one thing I was especially curious about. I asked my brothers.

"Why is it you boys aren't going to the Candor school, like Moosey?"

"Oh man, Pa would have none of it," said Ark. "He went down to the tax office about three or four times before they relented. For some reason Pa thinks we should be in the Ithaca schools. I'm not sure why he is so adamant. Or how he won in the end."

"When he pointed out that he pays taxes in this county, for the land on King Road, they had no choice. He threatened to withhold taxes," Sam chimed in. "They had to give in!"

We all laughed at the thought of Pa arguing with authority people. Each of us had seen his maximum wrath no more than a handful of times, but that was enough to banish any wish to risk seeing it again. Pa had an overall distrust of government. I kinda wondered if it's because of growing up under the sort of government like the Ottomans, which I was studying about in world history. Ark had another idea.

"I overheard him complain to Ma that the U.S. closed the doors to immigrants and left lots of people suffering back in the old country. He told her they were lucky to have gotten out when they did."

I especially felt sorry for Ark, my smart brother. He was hiding a secret. From everybody. But on one Friday earlier in the year, he'd let it out that the guidance counselor at the school was pushing him to apply for college. Well, Ma and Pa had saved, but they only had enough for one of the boys. They chose Mitch. He enrolled in Cornell that fall but had already left it after one semester. The money was used up. I don't know if that's why he left or if he flunked out. But I sure wish the money and the chance had been given to George. I have the feeling he would have made it work. I know he wanted it bad, but he kept it to himself, poor guy!

When my turn finally came, graduation felt festive. Maybe because their son Gifford graduated in the same year, Dr. Harry and Dr. Helen Bull not only attended the ceremony, but threw a little party afterwards. I know Pa was working, but it still felt like an excuse for my parents not to be there. I decided not to show my disappointment to anyone. We walked together across State Street and up College Avenue, a household of seven including me and Gifford in real gowns and caps that the school lent to us. We crossed the bridge over Cascadilla Gorge and on to Barnes Hall at Cornell—a peaceful, churchlike structure—where the ceremony took place. I didn't mind that I was the oldest of twenty graduates—only full of amazement that I was there at all!

My benefactors, having guided me toward my future this far, suggested I apply to nursing school programs at Alfred, Syracuse, and the University of Buffalo, but I felt trapped somewhere between elation and despair. I had no idea how I could afford to attend. For a while I let myself float along on the current of some sort of magical belief that when there is a will, there's a way… but it would come crashing down to reality at night when I tried to sleep. I couldn't muster the guts to broach the subject with the doctors. They've done so much for me; I had to figure this out for myself.

It took another year to save up. I worked at the Egan's grocery store and for a dentist, Dr. Fayhe; later on I worked for the Torbuts, too. I now paid $5 a week back to the doctor for my room and board. Finally my will found its way. The next August I took a suitcase with everything I owned on the train to Buffalo. The nursing school gave me room and board as an intern. Clearing and setting up trays at the school morphed into hospital work as an aid. The University of Buffalo partnered with the Edward J. Myer Hospital, which became my home.

The school paired me with two housemates: Vivian, a self-confident, regal sort of gal, was a year ahead of me and knew all the ropes; pretty Jean, a naïve, sweet girl, was so openhearted and easy going that I never experienced a tense moment. All my life, I had wanted two things: a doll and a girlfriend. The doll, I could buy myself. And now I had a best friend in Jean faster than you could count to three.

My savings didn't go far enough, since I had to pay $60 a subject ($30 in the summer sessions). So school was going to take a while. I needed another job to keep up tuition cost and keep my classes going as long as the school subsidized my board. I was mulling this over when I stopped into a little grocer's shop on my way home from a hospital shift. It was just before Christmas, and I was trying to decide if I should spend the train fare to go home over the school break or, instead, inquire about extra hospital shifts. Vivian and Jean would be with their families, and it would be a lonely holiday if I stayed on. My head was down, while I contemplated these things. The tiny store was so crowded with display items spilling onto the floor, it allowed for only one body at a time between rows.

Suddenly, a certain smell distracted me from my thoughts—zahtar! It was an herb that Pa and Ma grew and mixed, and put in everything, especially the coating on Pa's shankleesh cheese wheels. My feet propelled me toward the smell. It seemed to be coming from a counter with a display case of Arabic salads and pastries and... wouldn't you know it, a round, green-black zahtar-coated ball of shankleesh! The old man standing behind it barely cleared the top, he was so short and wizened. His face looked vaguely familiar. He was looking back at me and suddenly broke into a huge grin, then hustled around to the front of the display case to embrace me!

"Why, it's Suzee! Kee-feck, Suzee!" I stared and stared, chin dropped, at a loss. The man threw back his head and laughed at me. "Of course, what is wrong with me? No reason you should remember!" He launched into Arabic for a better command of the description.

"I was just a peddler and not doing very well when I walked to your family's farm in the hope of a rest. Your people fed me, put me to rest, and took me to the train depot in Ithaca. I can never forget! And now, one of those angels appears in my store and provides me with an opportunity to repay a kind favor. What can I do for you, my Suzee?"

Well! If this wasn't the... I had no words. But I managed to remind him that I was the inhospitable one of the family who had called him a bum and disobeyed my mother's command to feed him. This man—he only laughed even more and took my face in both his hands.

"Suzee, that is the way all children must grow. It is from the generosity of others that we learn to overcome our fear feelings and begin to trust in goodness. And here you are, meant to be once more in my life!" When I told him about my studies, he asked me what was in the way of my goals. I was honest with him.

He made it so easy. As it turns out, Mr. Abdulky was my very own angel. I went to work for him the next day, and I vowed to repay him for his grace. I stayed on through the summer and managed to knock out two extra courses while working, plus I got home for a week's vacation in August—at Mr. Abdulky's insistence. By fall, I felt indispensable to the store, and it was more and more difficult to fit in my hospital duties. There was growing need for more nurses, too, and rumors flying around that opportunities would be plentiful for nurses if the U.S. should enter the war. In December, we listened together, our foreheads touching as we bent over the little store radio; the announcer proclaimed in a booming voice what everyone who had come in and out all day was predicting. We were in! Mr. Abdulky didn't share my excitement. He said he saw too much war the last time and his eyes filled with sadness.

I worked hard for two years but there was fun in my life, too. The girls and I planned outings whenever we could, and swapped clothes and stories. Jean dated several boys, and her antics filled our lives with tales of drama, and sometimes led to a double date for me, too. Nothing that took, mind you. It didn't matter to me. For the first time in my life, I believed in my future. Things were working out okay for me when they suddenly got even better.

Man, what a buzz there was at the hospital on the morning of June 16th. I arrived for my shift just as a recruiting station was being propped up right next to the nursing station on the ground floor. Congress and FDR had passed a bill called the Bolton Act, and "The Meyer," my hospital, would be joining the training program; anyone could register in the Cadet Nursing Corps. I would continue my current program in an accelerated, challenging way for thirty-six months, fully subsidized for tuition, books, uniforms, and stipend! In exchange, we would pledge to "actively serve in essential civilian or federal government services for the duration of the war"—basically, serve our country as a nurse wherever needed. Two of my brothers, Jake and George, were already serving, and three more of them spoke of little else. I could pay for the balance of training and serve at the same time. Me, a girl. No question, I was all in!

We would receive $10 a month for the first year of training, $15 for the second, and $20 monthly in the third year, which corresponded with longer hours on hospital wards. For my first nine months, beginning July 1943, regulations allowed only twenty-four hours per week on the ward, so I continued at the store through the end of the year. Dear old Mr. Abdulky would have supported me in anything I chose, but he was especially proud of me as a Cadet Nurse and extolled my status to anyone who wandered into the store.

Vivian and Jean signed up, too. We were issued two uniforms: a gray woolen jacket-suit and velour overcoat for winter and a gray and white striped cotton suit and twill raincoat for summer. Man, these were stylish clothes, too. Our gray beret had a spread eagle and American shield and the same insignia patch was on the left shoulder of our cadet uniform and student nurse school uniform. You could not mistake a cadet nurse on the floor of any hospital. Posters showed up all over town, recruiting cadet nurses just like soldiers, so we girls strutted in our outside uniforms when we went out to the movies and basked in the attention and looks of approval, even admiration, from everyone around. For every year of the program we accumulated a silver button on our lapel, feeling the accomplishment deeply. And I, who could not carry a tune, pushed my lungs to the limit when I sang the Cadet Hymn at ceremonies:

> "Now I dedicate my service, pledge myself and all I am,
> Thus to make of life a triumph, over sorrow over death,
> Give me pride in my endeavor
> In the service of my Corps,
> O grant that I may heal
> The suffering ones!"

CHAPTER 10

LETTERS

South Danby - 1942

LAURA

Jake was the first to go. He left before spring, with March blowing around like more than the one lion in the saying. It was just before the 1942 season of the Danby Pirates would begin, which was ironic, because Pa had finally come around. Pa hadn't accepted Jake's talent as a ballplayer, and it seemed, for as long as I could remember, that he was perpetually "mad" at Jake. I guess 'cause Jake was always playing when Pa felt he should be working. In retaliation, Pa refused to attend any games or bless his playing; instead, he grumbled and shut down any conversation of it. But all of my brothers made a point to sneak off and watch Jake play whenever possible and, of course, I tagged along. The stretch of gravel in front of the barn was always filled with old cars the boys would constantly tinker with and at least one could usually be driven off to a game.

Last summer, of '41, was Jake's last season of ball and it sure was a blissful one—not too hot, although the air carried just enough sweetness of ripening fruit and berries along with the mid to late summer blooms. I am going to remember that summer to brighten all my future days, a time when we were still all together, and nobody had yet peeled away to leave me alone on a big old farm with Ma and Pa pining away for them. Ark was finally back to work, after months of healing broken bones in his vertebrae that he got from being thrown by the load truck while laying bricks on State Street Hill. By August his skin was as dark as the chestnut mare. Jake, John, and Mitch were all working at Morse Chain and driving their own cars. Sam just graduated from Ithaca High and worked with Ark for the summer but was going to start work as a milk tester in September. Susie came home twice that summer from Buffalo, and Moosey and I were free from school, but stuck with most of the milking.

On a perfect Saturday, late in the morning, we were all getting ready to drive down to pretty Stewart Park at Ithaca's lakeshore and watch Jake's semi-final game of the league. Susie had visited the week before and so was the only one of us missing that day. The chores were complete, Pa returned from Saturday rounds, Ma was canning berries and happy to be left alone for the afternoon, and I felt something fresh and different in the air. We were taking two cars to carry seven siblings. I watched John, Mitch, George, and Jake pile into John's Model A Ford, and I was about to climb in behind Sam and Moosey in Sam's car when something made me turn back and call, "Hey, Pa! It's a perfect day! Why not ride along with us? The lake breeze will be swell, and you can stroll around the park while we watch, if you want."

To everyone's surprise, Pa agreed. Moosey moved from the front to the back seat so Pa could sit up front, and Sam stepped on the gas, peeling out onto Peter Road, far behind our older brothers.

The games were always full of excitement, and this one was no different. The Pirates trailed by a few points until the ninth inning. I had noticed Pa walk out on the pier and then over to the boathouse to inspect the goings on in the inlet and across the water. Maybe the cracks of the wood bats against balls was too tempting to resist because from the corner of my eye, I saw him saunter back toward us and over to the cars lining the field's perimeter. He settled himself on the hood of Sam's Dodge, one leg tucked under his chin, a gob of snow-white hair blowing in multiple directions, and smoked his Camel cigarettes, one after another.

I think by that point we all noticed, but promptly forgot about, his presence at the bottom of the ninth with two outs and two on base. This would be the decisive moment in any game, and always exciting, but even more so because the Danby Pirates were down by two points. Jake was up to bat, and I believe now that eight Peters in that park, and maybe even Jake, collectively held our breath. The homerun surprised no one, considering Jake's talent and our unwavering belief that he would save the day, except probably Pa, who had never witnessed such moments of triumph in Jake's life: in fact, until this moment he had shunned any knowledge of them. But shock claimed the faces of every one of us in the park that day, including Jake, when our father jumped from the hood of that Dodge, tossed his cigarette aside and ran straight over to the diamond.

"Tat's my boy!" he whooped as loud as anyone ever heard him holler. "Tat's my boy!"

He was grinning ear to ear on the ride home. I asked him if he was proud of Jake.

"Tat, too," he said. Before I could vocalize the "huh?" that was forming on my lips, he mysteriously added, "Was tinking bout first time alone with your Ma…right tere in Renwick Park!" And that was clearly all he was gonna say about it, so I made a note to ask Ma later.

Jake enlisted on March 17th so none of us saw another season and, sadly, Pa missed out on all the potential pleasure. George and Mitch both registered on February 14th but George went to Elmira, instead of to the local Ithaca board with Mitch; he was hoping to enlist with the Air Corps. He was rejected because his eye vision could not be corrected to 20-20, so he waited for the draft and was inducted in August, with basic training in Atlantic City. Fortunately, George's aptitude test matched with the Air Corps' need of airplane mechanics and radio technicians, so he ended up in the Air Corps after all, and was sent to attend school for it in Lincoln, Nebraska. But before Ark left, we had a momentous event.

Pa often took us all to Geneva some weekends to visit Ma's cousins, Abe and Martha John. On one of those weekends, John met a nice Syrian girl named Charlotte Eassa, from Syracuse, who was visiting friends. The very first wedding in our family took place on June 14th, 1942. Naturally, we all went, except Jake who was already gone, and met a large community of Syrians in Syracuse. The huffla style wedding had live Syrian music—big city style, and we all danced to the ouds and dumbeks, even Pa who waved his handkerchief over his head from the front of the debke line. Sam and Mitch made a scene, they got so drunk, but nobody seemed to mind. George never stopped dancing, even though he and Sam had no rhythm at all, and I wasn't the only girl who giggled watching them. There were lots of Syrian girls I'd never met, whose eyes swept over my handsome brothers. Even my cousin, Maryanne John, was there, so I had my very own pal. What a swell party the Eassas threw!

At first John and Charlotte got a place at 142 Giles Street, across from the creek at the bottom of South Hill. John could walk straight up the hill to work from there. Later they moved a few blocks to Spencer Street and bought a house with an apartment to lease out. John came to the farm on Saturdays and Sundays to help out and sometimes Charlotte came, too, which made Ma happy.

It's springtime all over the world and, boy, do I love the spring in South Danby. It's so fragrant and fresh that sometimes it is easy to forget there's a war on. Each April, forsythia are everywhere in Ithaca; the yellow blossoms spill from the branches that line roads and driveways. These are Pa's favorites, but they are already gone this unusually warm May, and the lilacs have been in full bloom since the beginning of the month—Ma's favorites. We have two full bushes in the front of the house—the perfume follows me in and out—and they're Ma's pride and joy.

It's a lot quieter on our farm with just three brothers left in the house. This is especially true because Sam is gone for long days and a lot of times doesn't come home nights, driving all over the region from farm to farm. He tests milk for fat content for Caton Dairy Herd Improvement and is paid by the Farm Bureau, I think. He has to drive his old '34 Ford and stays over at the farms if they are far away. But Sam went to Syracuse to take an exam for the Air Corps and will be leaving soon, too.

Mitch went to Cornell for a semester; he was the one chosen by Pa and Ma to get the money for college, but I guess he didn't manage it or maybe he didn't like it. He's now on the assembly line at Morse Chain. Moosey switched from Candor High School to Ithaca and will graduate this year. I'm a junior and I ride to school with him, which is fun, but his old car breaks down a lot and strands us sometimes. He wants to enlist right after graduation, but Pa talked him into waiting a bit longer.

The other brothers are all either enlisted or registered, and still compare notes—believe it or not—about the scars that got recorded on their cards! You'd think these were badges of honor which every single one of 'em have. George's wrist scar is from the older boys branding him when they played cowboys on the old farm and he was too little to know better, but the rest of them got their "badges" on the fields or in the barn. It gives them lots of laughs.

I write a letter every day to either Jake or George and, since Jake was just home for furlough, tonight I wrote to Ark (that's our nickname for George). I told him how much Jake has changed, how sentimental he has gotten and how he already seems tired of the army. I told Ark how Ma said I can go to a party my girlfriend invited me to on the 26th. There will be square dancing and I will stay with her all night—just nine days from now so believe me, I'm counting!

I told Ark how warm this May has been and that we got the garden planted already, a fairly good-sized one right in the backyard below the house, across from the plum trees. Peas, lettuce, radishes, and green onions came out good. I wrote:

"We planted early potatoes, plowed up the strawberries behind the milk house, and moved quite a few of them to the other garden below the barn, where we have onions already and will plant the tomatoes and peppers. Our apricot, peach, cherry, plum, and apple trees have all blossomed well and we expect a good year for fruit. Ma says she is going to can a lot because, by the time the war is over, there'll be use for it. It's been so warm that Ma took off her long underwear (I thought maybe you would be amused), but it got cool today, so she put on Sam's coveralls and now she likes long pants and says she's going to wear them all the time. She looks nice in them, but Pa just laughed at her."

But mostly, I told my brother to write more about the angel he found, his Gloria. She is a college student he met in Lincoln; it was a blind date his buddies set up through their wives who work with Gloria at a department store. Her grandma runs a barber shop by herself—imagine that! He is head over heels for her, but he got transferred to Williams Air Base in Arizona just a few months after he met her, and is pining away for this girl—poor Ark! I feel for him.

I read every word to Pa and Ma, and Ma shook her head but oddly, she didn't complain. Ma has respect for love and always told us how she defied her villagers by marrying Pa, who had to take them all on. But she is real strong about us marrying Syrians, at best, or Armenians, at the very least. So I expected her to be upset with Ark. Maybe she thinks it won't last.

I signed off the letter and then had Ma sign which made me remember the most important thing I had to tell my brother!

"P.S. Guess what, Ark! Sam and I taught Ma how to write her name. She practiced and practiced and is so proud about it you would laugh your head off! As you can see above, we taught her the English version—Helen Peter! We asked her if she wanted to learn to write her Syrian name, Haloun, and she said, 'What for? I don't know how to write it in Syrian even. May as well move on...'"

For my senior year, without Moosey to ride with, I had no way to go to school because Pa stopped working at the plant; with all the farm work and milking to do alone, he couldn't be driving me back and forth either. Charlotte and John have a new baby—my first niece, Vicky. Since Charlotte could use help, the perfect solution was for me to live-in with John and Charlotte at their new place on Spencer Road during the week, walk to school, and help with the baby after school. Pa picks me up every Friday in his old Star car to go home on the weekends. They are awful lonely without me since I'm the only one left. But most of all, they can't read the letters and postcards that arrive from my brothers.

Sam enlisted last February and has already finished radio school in Wisconsin; he is now stationed at March Field in

California. He wrote after he had a nice furlough and visited Uncle Archie in Los Angeles. This was special because Sam is more of a postcard kind of guy and as much as he likes to talk, he doesn't write many words. We got postcards from Wisconsin and now a postcard from L.A. tucked inside. But he must have been excited to have written a whole letter. I read it to Pa and Ma:

"Dearest little Sis Zaha, boy did I have a great time at Uncle Archie's. He took me all over the city. First he showed me his flower shop in downtown, where I met Uncle Leo for the first time. Boy, is he a short wiry guy, only comes up to my shoulders! And he has a wooden leg, too, but I guess Pa and Ma already know that. Cousin Nishan is already thirteen and is getting so big. Horon and Eddie, Satinique's sons, are real swell guys. Their dad was killed in Turkey in the last war trying to escape but they made it here, thank goodness for Uncle Archie since Aunty Satinique is real sweet and hospitable. She's been through a lot and talks about things that Pa never discusses, things back in Turkey. Give my love to Ma and Pa and I'll write again real soon. Tell Ark I miss him when you write to him, and want to meet up with him when our furloughs match." Pa only grunted at Sam's words, but Ma beamed from ear to ear.

Mitch enlisted in March, which we all expected. But then Moosey went off and did it— Pa acted mad as hell, but I think he is just plain scared with the last one of his sons gone. And since Moosey went to the army, we are holding our breath he doesn't go into the infantry and see action. He left on April 8th to Fort Dix and got hospitalized just one month later. We know because he wrote a letter to Ma and Pa during this period. But then he was discharged from the hospital and his last letter told us he was on his way overseas which threw our parents into panic like I've never seen before. We know where the other boys are: Mitch is a mechanic and crew member for the Army tugboat division. George is still at Williams Air Field and working on P-38s and B-17s. He wrote the most at first, but now he writes less often since he is writing to Gloria almost daily. Jake is also a mechanic and crew chief in the Army Air Corps; he works on B-26 aircraft at Fort Bragg, North Carolina. I guess these brothers of mine are putting all their tinkering to use for the country. But Moosey… we just don't know where Moosey is.

He doesn't—or can't—write. We know from the radio news that there is lots of action over there. Pa rushes through the milk deliveries and sits on a chair in the front yard between the chestnut tree and one of the lilac bushes every afternoon. Why? He waits for the postman and God help me if I'm not nearby when a letter is delivered.

"Zaha! Come quick!" he roars at me, his hand shaking when he hands me the letter. But I am only home on the weekends. Sometimes poor Pa and Ma wait up to three days for me to read whatever letter had arrived during the week. One time Pa was too anxious to wait and drove all the way to John's house, bursting through the door and waking the baby, for me to read the letter. One Saturday I was picking cherries in the orchard and he went berserk until his frantic eyes found me. He came running down to the orchard, waving the letter over his head and was out of breath when we sat down under the tree so I could read. Normally, Pa would pace while I read, acting like I couldn't read fast enough for him but then, when he asked me to read a letter again, I would laugh in his face. Pa usually laughed back but still made me read it through a second time. When I sat at the little table in the parlor to write to the boys, both Ma and Pa, who almost never enter the parlor under other circumstances, found excuses to constantly pass by me.

"Tell George about ta tomatoes..." or "Tell Sam I fix ta radio again…"

In June a letter came from Chi Chi, which I read to Pa and Ma on the back porch; she wrote for her mother, who wanted Pa to know her Hagop has also gone, deployed to Europe on the ships. It felt like the whole world went into waiting and we held our collective breath. There were now five star stickers on our front window—one for each son in the service. Ma was so proud of those stars, she often washed down the window around them, to be sure they stood out, good and visible from the roadside.

This meant, of course, that there was no one left when my high school graduation came. But graduate I did! It was a swell ceremony. Susie could not get time off from the hospital, so she sent me a card. The boys had all had their special day, but they were far away now; it was bittersweet to be graduating alone. Pa and Ma came to the big basketball hall at Cornell University to watch me march in my cap and gown. From my spot in the middle of the seated class, I turned to find them hunched together on the glistening wooden bleachers. They looked dwarfed but I could tell they were real proud of me. Susie told me later, "Gee, ya'd think you were the first daughter they ever had graduate high school!" and I could tell she was jealous or mad, but what could I say? I suppose Pa and Ma didn't go to hers.

When we got home from the ceremony, I got the best graduation surprise you ever could imagine! My honey bunch brother Ark was sitting on the front step in his sharp Airs Corps uniform, grinning like a Cheshire cat and looking like a movie star. In fact, I thought, I must be in a movie right now. Ma and I both screamed at the top of our lungs and flew out the car doors before Pa had put the parking gear in place. We barely let him move his legs to get inside the house, we were hanging on him. Then he embraced Pa and they looked so happy, that when they turned to smile at us, their arms wrapping one another's shoulder, I snapped a picture with my new camera—a graduation present from Susie! George was absolutely giddy.

"Sorry to take you by surprise, but the furlough was so last minute, I didn't have time to even get off a telegram. And besides, I have a mission to focus on," with those last words, he winked at me and grinning slyly, waited for the questions that were about to fly at him.

"Okay, okay! The fact is, I made a stop in Lincoln on my way...." More grins and a long pause. Man, he was really milking our suspense. Finally, "I proposed to Gloria!"

George planned to buy a ring in town and meet Gloria at the train stop in St. Louis, on his way back to Arizona, to give it to her. I couldn't imagine a more romantic thing in the world. And he let me go downtown with him to shop for it. It was only mid-afternoon and Pa and Ma decided to go to town, too, so we all piled in. Our parents wandered the downtown blocks like little kids—I even wonder if they ever did anything like this before—while Ark and I hit the pavement like sleuths. There were a heck of a lot of jewelry stores within three blocks downtown, not even counting the department stores that George wanted no part of.

First, we cased out each store and studied the window displays. Then we went inside Chandler's, Hill's, Patten's, Rudolph Brothers', and Schooley's. Finally, my brother went back to Patten's for his selection, an understated but elegant band of white gold with a modest square diamond flanked by two smaller stones. He said it was perfect—that it matched her sweet personality. We met up with Ma and Pa and drove on to Cayuga Street to Betty's for ice cream, and Pa toasted us both with his vanilla ice cream cone—our special day! It was dampened by one thing only. We heard the news about the Normandy Landing on June 6th, and wondered if Moosey's platoon was in those boats. It was a safe bet he was over there.

"What you think, George?" Pa asked.

"It's not likely you'll hear from him out of France, so don't assume the worst," Ark told Ma and Pa. "The timing of the transport fits with the completion of his basic training, so he's there, no doubt. And no news right now is good news."

After a long half year without my brothers, Christmas of 1944 sure was lonely. I did my best to cheer my folks. Ma and I cooked stuffed grapeleaves and we had a lovely time, but so much sighing went on that Pa scolded Ma for it and told her she was making things worse. I'll tell you what was really worse—the short days that followed in January and February, that's what. Those days were so blustery and cold it was an agony even getting to the barn for the milking. Either the wind howled and hollered at our windows or the top of our hill fell into a silent hush of whiteness; you never knew which way you preferred it, but typically not what you got at the moment.

Now it was all up to Pa and me to keep the cows milked and fed. He thinned out the herd somewhat so he could handle it. We had put up enough canning for the winter and we took some down to poor Aunt Mary Moses whose boys were all gone to the war, too. All her boys had changed their last name to Mike while they were still in high school (and I don't know why) but Pa and Ma still referred to her as Mary Moses. We made sure to take her milk, too. As for milk, it was in high demand and Pa felt obligated to get it out the door. And lots of the Syrians came up to the farm for milk. It was hard to get in town. The rations meant we couldn't get much sugar, but Pa still baked, and the berries and peaches Ma put up in the fall lasted us through the winter with extra to give away. We couldn't complain like some folks.

The first week in January, we got dumped with snow and winds picked up hard. On Wednesday, the snows had drifted so bad the road was covered. We were used to this; Pa would hitch the horse to the milk cart and drive the field to South Danby Road through the places where the snow had blown away into drifts blocking the road. When John came up early Saturday mornings, a few times they tried driving the team straight down Singer Hill but one day they wiped out—spinning not once, but three times going down—and came to a stop halfway off the bridge. John had been driving and he laughed when he described Pa's sense of humor in that scary moment. In the silent moment afterwards, Pa had turned to him and said, "Man, that was some fancy driving!"

When Pa had to take the car to work, he put ropes on the tires to drive through deep snow. The gray sky was filled up with a cloud blanket that just hung, menacing, and my face stung something fierce from the brutal wind when I ran, fast as I could, to the barn. After the milking was done and delivered, we hunkered down near the stove to a hot lunch of loobi stew, pilaf, and hunks of Pa's bread. After, I settled down in the parlor to write to some of the boys while Ma did some sewing by the stove. I barely noticed the door open, other than the howl that roared abruptly like a switch that turned on when it opened and off when it closed. I assumed Pa had stepped out to check on the cows. But when my hands were too cramped up to write another word and I stacked the pages I had finished, it occurred to me he hadn't come back in. Ma and I were both worried.

Another hour passed before he stumbled in the door, pushed by a strong wind like it was scolding him to get inside. We did just that—scolded him for being out so long and he shushed us, growling, "Tat's what Kennet Traver said. I told him, 'You wouldn't understand! You don't have five sons in ta armies! Gotta know tey is okay.'"

When the roads get this bad, the mailman can't get through. When there are letters, he was in the habit of leaving them for us at Fred Hill's place on the South Danby Road, about two miles down from Peter Road. Pa had walked through the drifts and wind all that way and back to see if there was any letter! It was worth the hike for him, since there was a letter from Jake, which he shoved into my hand to read. The three of us sat down around the stove so Pa could quickly warm up and I started:

"Dear Pa, Ma, and Zaha. I got my furlough approved in two weeks and will be bringing my girl, Hazel. We arrive Jan 20…." The three of us looked up and back and forth at one another, amazed. This was the first we heard of… Hazel.

CHAPTER 11

BRIDES FOR BROTHERS

Ithaca - 1945

LAURA

1945 was a big year for our family, and not just because the war ended. Deep in the darker days of February, just when I worried Pa could never make it through the winter not knowing when or if he would see my brothers again, I could have kissed John for the cheer he brought Pa. For a long time, John usually came up on weekends on his day off to help with the farm chores that couldn't get done during the week, especially in hay season. But he and Charlotte had just moved to Syracuse to open a little grocery store, so couldn't get away too often anymore. One snowy Saturday that month we sat down to eat a special dinner because Charlotte also came for the day. We were having a swell time together.

Anyway, John and Pa got to talking about the war and then John said, "You know, Pa, you really ought to apply to be a U.S. citizen now. It's time."

"Nah, I tried to do it. At Highland Park, went with Ameen. Tey ask too many questions."

"So what? What have you got to be afraid of? Especially now you have five sons serving for the country, they'd be glad to have you." And John took a day off that week to meet Pa downtown. They went to the county courthouse where John filed the papers for him. When Pa came home, he was floating! He couldn't stop shaking his head in amazement.

"Just like tat! Henna told ta guy I have ta five sons in military. Ta man looked at me right in my eye. Ten he said, 'We need more citizens like you!' And went stamp, stamp, stamp on ta paper!" Pa was grinning from ear to ear after he mimicked the man's words in his broken English. He looked over at the five stars in our window that he was so proud of and smacked a kiss to them. All three of us laughed and giggled through supper that night. Every so often Pa shook his head in amazement and sort of whispered, "Amirkan!"

Then my honey bunch brother Ark wrote that he finally got his furlough approved so he and his beloved Gloria set a wedding date in Lincoln. The best part is that they were to marry on June 11th—my birthday! I was so happy for Ark, I knew from his letters he was mad with love for Gloria, and I couldn't wait to meet the vision of a perfect woman he described. I decided to practice calling him George instead of his nickname, now that he was a married man and Ark would not do.

But then he sent another letter just before the wedding that his furlough was extended enough days that he decided to bring Gloria home to meet the family. They caught a train the same night, right after the reception, and the next night

Pa picked them up so late that we just rushed them off to bed. We assured them we would make our acquaintance with Gloria in the morning, after they got a chance to rest. Ma burst into tears after they went upstairs—happily, not in front of Gloria, but Pa and I were at a loss.

"What kind of farm woman can she be—she's so little!" wailed Ma. Pa just laughed at her, but I felt real bad for Gloria. George has written extensively about how she is the sweetest woman on earth, and Ma is worrying about her size? None of us are any taller, for goodness sake. Ma, least of all!

Gloria won her over instantly, as she did every single person she would ever meet. Her hair is white-blonde, lighter than the heads of Finns and Swedes around here. And those big blue eyes know only how to smile, like a clear summer sky. What really impressed me was Gloria's nature. How can someone come into this house with all the guttural Syrian talk around you, which you can't understand a word of, and still smile patiently and calmly, just waiting your turn to be addressed? I know none of us in this family would ever have that kind of patience! And when Ma discovered that Gloria's hands were perfect for slipping in and out of the pickling jars when she helped with the jams that week, all crisis was averted! Ma guessed Gloria would do. We've come a long way from Ma's insistence on us all marrying one of our own, like John did. I suppose that's what war can do to change the old ways.

George and Gloria left for an even longer train ride home; they had to report back to George's base at Roswell, New Mexico and settle into new married housing. I hated to see them go—who knows when we'll see them? We had a picnic the next day, just like old times: the Syrians came from Tubbha, the Johns from Geneva, and some of Pa's cousins came from Binghamton. Ma said it was to celebrate the end of the war in Europe and three sons married, and just, well—happiness, I guess! It was like a big sigh of relief for Pa and Ma when that summer kicked off. Almost every son was alive and accounted for, soon to be discharged from military service. Except for one missing link, and it was eating at Ma something awful.

Moosey was over in Europe since the big fight we kept hearing about, but we still hadn't heard from him since June. You can imagine Ma up nights wailing and Pa shushing her to stay calm. I could tell he was trying hard not to obsess like her, but he was scared, too. When we finally did get some word, it was in an unexpected way, and I wrote to tell George about it. A guy who said he had worked with George at Ithaca Gun in '42 drove up to the house one day and asked Ma if she was Mrs. Peter, mother of Moses. Ma about fainted, she was so afraid of bad news, and the guy sensed this and real fast said, "Mrs. Peter, I only came to pay my respects and congratulations!" Then he sat down with Pa and Ma and me and told us he grew up in Slaterville Springs, which is about the same distance east of Ithaca as South Danby is south. He had been in a German POW camp when a platoon of American soldiers came in and liberated them, just a couple of months earlier. It was a great sight to see them burst into camp, he said.

"This real little guy was leading them. He had guns hanging from both sides, ammunition belts strapped across both shoulders—you could hardly see his body under all that!"

he said. "The first thing this guy says is, 'All right you lazy bums, your vacation is over!'"

After that, Moosey had asked if anyone was from Ithaca, New York which shocked this guy and he gratefully identified himself. Pa and Ma couldn't be prouder, but it sure was a curious image of our Moosey, the way this guy described him. We did get one postcard finally, in June, in which he said he was on a little R&R and got to a place to mail something. But after that—radio silence. Not another word. My parents struggled to celebrate all the good things happening to the rest of us while worrying that Moosey could be hurt or... worse. We waited all of July and August. It was one very long summer. We heard from Martha that Hagop (Jack) was not yet back either.

I got a job at Tompkins Trust Company, and Pa had been driving me there and back, which was getting hard on him. Mitch came home, followed by Sam. Mostly we waited on Moosey and prayed. Ma dug the potatoes. Pa drove the milk to the creamery. John still came on weekends to help. George and Gloria waited in Roswell for George's discharge. We all began to get punchy—nervous, I guess. If he was alright, why would he not write? Was he…?

At the end of summer—I think it was the first of September—we heard someone hollering and honking outside; Fred Hill came racing up the hill. He must have been in some hurry since he was out of breath when the car stopped short and he scrambled out.

"Joe, Joe! Mose is coming. He's soon to arrive at Ithaca!" The only neighbor with a telephone, he had gotten the call.

Ma squealed, genuflected, and pulled on Pa, dragging him to the Star. I jumped in, too. I couldn't breathe and my heart was racing. We didn't think to grab anything, which didn't matter—it was so hot that first day of September. Pa's driving couldn't satisfy Ma.

"Faster, faster!" she nagged, even screamed at him all twelve miles to the train depot. I thought she would have a heart attack. When we peeled into the space by the platform and climbed out, we saw him immediately. He was strolling toward us with the biggest, most mischievous grin, and I just wanted to wrap my arms around him for the joy rising inside me.... But I had to jerk my head away because Ma fainted right next to us—Pa and I barely caught her.

Moosey had sailed home on the *Queen Elizabeth*, imagine that! He said they were treated like royalty on the boat. It took me a long time to find out anything about Moosey's war, and only from my other brothers. He didn't talk about it, but when I washed his army pants one day I found a hole in them. I asked Moosey what the hole was from and he nonchalantly said it was a bullet hole, like that was the most normal thing in the world. He couldn't see my face go white as he walked away, but the way I felt, I knew all color must have left me. Sam told me Moosey and one other guy had gotten separated from their unit. Not knowing where their unit was, they went ahead and crossed a river. They didn't know the rest of their unit had been killed.

Sam told me, "They found out later they were the first Americans to cross the Rhine River into Germany!"

And Mitch told me, "His buddy was shot and killed right by his side while they were moving..."

But nothing else would be said and Moosey was known to be punchy after that.

With our little big family complete, it was about to grow even bigger. John and Charlotte had a second girl, and Jake and Hazel bought a house down on South Albany Street and had a little girl. Ma now had three sweet granddaughter babies to fuss over. They were American babies—Vicky, Lorraine, and little Joanie—but she did not complain one bit. George found out he had to report to Santa Ana, California to await discharge, so he and Gloria left Roswell for Los Angeles and stayed with Uncle Archie and sweet Auntie Satinique, my favorite aunt and uncle, lucky them! And with Jake, Mitch, Sam, and Moosey all home, the worst days were behind us.

Now I saved telling the beginning for the last, because the year 1945 began with a surprise for Pa that no one ever expected. When Jake came home that January, he brought his fiancée Hazel Robertson, a jolly red-headed girl from the south, with twinkly eyes and a no-nonsense personality. She was an important army nurse and she outranked Jake—she was a lieutenant! They met when he was hospitalized with appendicitis and had surgery, only a couple of months earlier. First, he went into the hospital in September and stayed in for a month. They discharged him but I guess he got worse because back he went in November and this time they operated and kept him until December. I think Hazel was the one who decided to operate since he didn't improve. They didn't know each other long; it must have been a powerful impact she had on him.

I always wondered why they chose to come to Ithaca to get married, instead of Hazel's home in Union, South Carolina.

Later, Susie told me she thought maybe it was because southern people are very prejudiced against outsiders and may not have taken kindly to Jake's foreign look and gruff manner. They may have wanted to give a little time for adjustment. In the war, it seemed all kinds were mixing and folks back home just didn't understand immediately.

Hazel's southern way was charming, and I liked her right away, though Susie did not. I think she felt jealous of Hazel's nursing experience; she already had accomplished what Susie worked so hard for. Hazel had a heck of a time adjusting to our cooking, though, and she kept some of her favorite foods in the bedroom. This also made Susie grumble when she came home to visit, but I thought, why not, poor thing? She must feel like she landed on Planet Mars here in the Peter household of loud and louder voices, all in a foreign language. I did what I could to make her feel welcome. She was to be my second sister-in-law, which brings me back to the beginning of this memorable year.

When Jake showed up with Hazel, they wanted to get married during their furlough. Well, our Methodist Church on South Danby Road had closed, because of the war, I guess. That's when I found out Pa grew up as a Presbyterian! Because of missionaries, he said. It was Saturday and I had come home to the farm for the weekend. Pa, Jake, and Hazel got in the car and I got in with them for something to do, and Pa drove us down into Ithaca and parked in front of the First Presbyterian Church. I was worried it would be closed and nobody would be there. There is a small green door at the Court Street side of the church. I guess Pa figured that would be the likely door to be functioning on a non-Sunday and he knocked at the door. A nice man wearing a reverend's collar answered and asked, "May I help you?"

Pa began to talk in his English but Jake interrupted him in Arabic, saying, "Let me talk, Pa. It will go easier!"

"I can talk for myself, damn it!" Pa retorted and turned back to the man standing there. But the man was gaping at him.

Then he sort of shook his head to break a spell and asked, "Are you from Syria? I recognize that accent. I lived there as a boy."

"Yes, sir. I am from Kasab and Ladehkiya. My name is Joe Peter."

"Kessab! Lattakia! That is where I lived," the man was getting excited. "Possibly... Did you go to the mission school?"

Now Pa was staring, quiet, and—I think—disbelieving. Then he spoke real slow, first in Arabic, then in another language, Kessab-talk, I guess. "Yes, both schools. My name is—was Hovsep Karamardian..." And the man, this minister—now he was crying!

"I am Walter, Hovsep! Do you remember me?" The words came out in gasps between his sobs. I'd never before seen Pa embrace a man who wasn't Armenian like Uncle Archie or his relatives. They both cried and seemed at a loss for words. We just stood there, Jake and Hazel and me, not knowing what to do. We knew we were witnessing something important, but we'd never thought about Pa as a boy, in the old country. I tried, really tried to imagine Pa like, about ten years old. The idea of it seemed so—well, foreign! *Odar*—a word Pa sometime used, but I don't think it was a Syrian word 'cause Ma never used it and she spoke enough about strangers, believe you me!

Reverend Dodds (Walter) would only be able to perform Jake and Hazel's nuptials within the next two hours. He was fully booked from that Saturday night right up until Monday when the couple's train would take them back to their bases in the Carolinas: Jake to the AAF base in Florence, and Hazel now stationed at Fort Bragg. So the four of us went straight to the Reverend's home and had the ceremony right then and there. I witnessed for Hazel and Pa stood up for Jake. After that Pa took us all to supper at Mr. Abbott's restaurant in Collegetown, but first he drove all the way to the farm to pick up Ma.

To celebrate even more, we decided to go to the pictures, but nobody could agree on which one. *Winged Victory* was playing at the Strand, but Jake and Hazel did not want to see a war movie on their vacation. There were three other choices, so Pa said we should give the bride final say and Hazel chose *Arsenic and Old Lace* at the Temple because she has a thing for Cary Grant. That ended a swell day, and we all rode home in the darkness to South Danby feeling satisfied, but the miracle of it seemed to stay with Pa a long time. When he dropped me off at the bank Monday morning, after leaving Jake and Hazel at the train station, Pa was still shaking his head and chuckling to himself. He muttered something in Armenian that included the name 'Walter,' so I asked him what he was thinking about. He looked over at me but it didn't seem like he was seeing me. From whatever place he was in, he vaguely answered, switching back to Syrian, "Can it be so long ago?"

INTERLUDE

ORPHANED

Ithaca - 2008

AUTHOR

Nobody was prepared for the death of my father in 2008—least of all, me. He left just three years after my mother. While her passing was expected—a long, protracted illness—his was not. A surgery that meant to resolve kidney issues led to a discovery of a more serious nature—with no solution and little time, only three or so weeks, as it happened. When my father learned how imminent the end was, he was angry at first, and panicked. He had three book projects to get published and was desperate to see them through. I took on the responsibility to carry out those missions for him, and often pray that I honor my promise to him.

His leaving was sudden and devastating. I suspect that for anyone of any age who has experienced unconditional love from their parents, becoming an orphan may be the most profound of all of life's transitions; for some, equal to becoming a parent.

I was at the ripe age of fifty-five, now adrift with no anchor. All that is right in the world—the knowing in one's core that all is as it should be—vanished with my father's last breath. In the case of George and Gloria Peter, the world had truly been a better place with them in it. This is still proclaimed and reaffirmed by so many they had touched and inspired, and who felt the loss deeply.

Until that moment, motherhood had been the most profound change to my identity and sense of being. Now my world was rocked and, it felt, violently so. For me, it completely splintered. As long as at least one of my parents walked the earth, I was protected, rooted, still part of a tribe—and loved. I thought I had wandered into a pathetic cliché when I stood in front of my bedroom window soon after and heard myself ask out loud to the world outside, "Does this mean I have to learn to love myself?"

Of course, the answer was obvious. But the "cliché" was no trite joke to me. I knew with clarity in that moment just how lazy my life had been, basking in the unconditional love that was always there for the taking, lazy about needing or developing other love—other intimate knowledge—and taking too much for granted to do the work needed to explore my own soul. Released into unknown space, I was forced—or free—to discover myself. (I know, I know. The clichés are endless.) My parents, whose protection had held me, now gifted me a new place in the world. It was time to do the scary work—this time for myself. The new aloneness triggered an instinct of self-preservation and ultimately turned me to the ancestors;

it felt the most natural way to maintain connection with the knowledge of my existence, my raison d'etre, if you will.

But I didn't get there immediately. My habit was to fill my life with busyness and self-perceived value. I was operating a B&B, teaching a full slate of voice students, raising a child alone, and producing a weekly concert series radio broadcast that took more of my time than everything else combined. So what did I do first? An orphan without a parent to fill my attention gap in any of my rare weekly off-hours? I seriously considered entering a Ph.D. program in ethno-musicology. I discussed it at length with a few professors I had partnered with. Then, I did something totally out of character for me. A practical exercise for a non-practical gal. I drew a line down a sheet of paper to "see" what my life might look like on the other side of the endeavor. In one column, I listed the activities that would fill my life after completion of a doctorate in my sixties: job searching for temporary teaching positions (too old to expect anything permanent), negotiating one- or two-year teaching contracts, the necessary moves to settle at universities around the world and all the logistics that would entail. My functioning life would leave room for little else.

In the opposite column, I listed what I wanted to do in my life that would not, could not happen, in this scenario. The list contained one prominent item in large, block letters: the book I wanted—needed—to write. Jido's story, the Karamardian story (plus some other stories cradled in my head for later). I stared at the list and saw the unwritten "either/or" between the columns. None of it could happen in tandem with the studies program. I had to nail down what mattered. A no-brainer, immediately obvious, I committed fully to the ancestors. I went directly to where I had begun as a pre-teen: this "Armenian" thing. I would pick up the story. Maybe I could find my way through it.

A framed poster hung on the family dining room wall since I can remember. It contained a printed quote by the famous author William Saroyan, and seemed the kind of item that was as common to Armenian home décor as was say, a camel saddle in the living room of 1950s and '60s Lebanese/Syrian homes, or a gold crucifix above a bed in any devout Catholic home. Our poster read:

"*Go ahead, destroy Armenia. See if you can do it. Send them into the desert without bread or water. Burn their homes and churches. Then see if they will not laugh, sing, and pray again. For when two of them meet anywhere in the world, see if they will not create a new Armenia.*"

Through my father's distress, I felt reminded with clarity, that I had made a personal promise to myself and the greater family, and I had postponed it for far too long. We discussed this in his final days, but mostly I clung to it as a harbor to reach for, beyond the ocean of loss that was drowning me. The quest to tackle the family story was more than passion and promise: it was lifesaving. It was clear now that the thing I most needed to accomplish before the end of my own days was a search for meaning through the motivations of my ancestors. Why, I cannot say. But somehow what they sought, thought, fought for, and felt, seemed intimately connected to me and my own path—as if I would discover answers I needed from them, even while I had no idea what the questions might be.

Joe Peter, his siblings, and family members had rearranged their physical world to find, and to create, what they needed in order to thrive. Once in America, Jido moved his family around Michigan, and to and from New York, always reaching for a piece of land on which he could provide for his family's needs, move his dreams forward, send his offspring on to greener pastures. They kept dreaming and, it seems, passed the dreams on. Perhaps, if I could identify the dreams and then work out how their lives progressed and triumphed, I might find where I fit in the process. Which brought me back to the Armenian question. In *Passage to Ararat*, Michael Arlen wrote:

"*All my life Armenia and Armenians had been a part of a dream; it and they were OUT THERE somewhere, hazy, nearly invisible. Now I was traveling into the dream. I would see what I would see. I would find what I would find.*"

This was the attitude I packed when I embarked on what I call 'My Big Fat Armenian Cruise' in 2009. Now fifty-six years old, I took the suggestion of my Los Angeles cousins to participate in an annual Armenian Heritage Cruise in the Caribbean that attracted Armenians the world over. Ever since I met my newly discovered, extended Karamardian family, I had marveled at the immersed cultural world in which most Armenians lived: Armenian school, Armenian church, Armenian social events, etc. This was a life I could not imagine. But, though I grew up oblivious to such a life, in some way I now felt deprived. I laugh now, recalling how my cousin Sossi had once adamantly exclaimed that she would not marry an Armenian. Her comment reminded me of a family wedding in Syracuse, filled with Syrian and Lebanese members of the Orthodox

Church, and a moment when my Aunt Charlotte had called out, "Denice, please come here. I want you to meet a nice Syrian boy!" I, of course, ran in the opposite direction and ducked into the ladies room until the coast cleared.

Ironically, my dear cousin Sossi fell deeply in love with an Armenian boy at university, a filmmaker, with whom she has enjoyed a long, creative, happy, and lasting marriage. Ever since we met in our twenties, I have wondered what my life would have been like had I grown up in the culture. A vague sense that this question might be a starting point drove me onboard that ship. I thought the cruise might offer the opportunity to glimpse what such a life would look like, from my position as an observer.

It was the most thrilling, total immersion into the culture I could have hoped for. I witnessed joy and contentment among intergenerational family groups that included babies in strollers, millennial couples, parents and grandparents, interacting over meals and poolside relaxation. They came from as far away as France, Australia, Canada, and Argentina. There were organized dancing lessons, meetings, and excursions. I took a stab at the Armenian line dances, much more sophisticated and flowing than the up and down motion of the Syrian debke with its jerky stomps and hops that I was accustomed to from our local Syrian hufflas.

I was one of only two students in the Armenian language class, which left me feeling as helpless as it did the other student—the non-Armenian spouse of someone. We were the only two non-speakers among 1,800 Armenians aboard. The people, these strangers from my fellow race (or, in my case, partial race), were gorgeous. Long black, flowing hair atop slim bodies and demure, soft-spoken voices was the signature look of the young women, animated conversation among the shorter middle aged and elderly, and intelligent faces on all. Music poured from three or four clubs at any given time. I would creep my way in or just peep from doorways at the dance floors filled with jubilant, moving Armenian bodies.

I was thrust into something new for me: the stark contrast of being on the outside looking in. In spite of the warm efforts by my roommate and her family to include me in their activities, I felt so removed from the energy around me that, in order to benefit from the experience, I resorted to an old acting skill. It involved "observing" a desired activity as if I were a reporter presenting a preview of a unique culture. Through the tour company, I had signed up to share a cabin. I was matched with an exuberant opera singer from Beirut, then living in Pasadena. Her sisters were also onboard, one from Montreal and one from Los Angeles, along with their spouses. They may have been in their seventies and were enjoying a rare and wonderful reunion together.

Elise taught me some Komitas songs on the balcony of our cabin and pointed out the talent and lack of skills of various singers we listened to in the ship concerts. I trailed her and her sisters on excursions to beaches and markets. They laughed richly in the upper bass tones of cellos, from deep in the gut, and approached life with a jolly gusto that made me homesick for the now missing generations of my own family.

Mostly, I wandered the ship and observed—literally, studied—"Armenians." The humbling, heavy dose of culture drenched in unfamiliar language (even Arabic has a familiar, if not intelligible, ring to my ears, having heard it so often as a child) threw my senses into perpetual overload. I have lived immersed within Spanish and Portuguese speaking countries, once had a decent command of French, even studied German and Italian. But the fact that the Armenian language is foreign to me fills me with shame and sadness. I can't help but wonder whether my Jido, who spoke at least six languages and wrote in both Arabic and Armenian alphabets, felt shame regarding his inferior command of English? A natural symptom of the *odar*? (which felt like my own status in this moment).

I found myself regularly seated at dinner with a group of Armenians from Glendale California. A doctor at the table seemed to seamlessly slip into a role of host/moderator, dominating and guiding the conversation each night. He enjoyed expounding on all things Armenian and made a point to educate me about Glendale: how 60-70% of its residents are Armenian (I had not known this). One evening, I found myself watching as if from above as I proceeded down a rabbit hole he gleefully dug for me. It began with an innocent question,

"Denice, are you married?'

"No."

"Were you ever married?"

"Yes."

"To an Armenian?"

"No."

He allowed for an appropriate pause, a pregnant silence that I sensed served as a warning. I somehow knew where he would lead, yet felt helplessly pulled along the path.

"Do you have siblings?"

"Yes. Two sisters and a brother."

"Married?"

I couldn't help but hesitate, seeking the right words as if I was supposed to explain. I ticked off each case in my head. Every one of us had divorced by that point, though one sister had recently entered into her third marriage. Somehow, he managed to plow through each case individually:

"Armenian?"

"No."

The exercise was repeated pointedly, like a courtroom presentation of evidence of pattern. With every no answer (there had been four of us, in total, exposed to have married non-Armenians and failed at each and every marriage), he looked around the table smugly and conspicuously nodded his unspoken message: "See? See what happens?"

Never mind that I wanted to screech at him, "*There were no Armenians in my town. No Armenians in my world! We didn't grow up in Glendale!*" I was unable to find my voice. I choked on the blatant manipulation exposing my life failures and my inability to defend myself, not to mention, the pointlessness of it. What was there to defend, anyway? Why should I feel accused of something?

This was part of being Armenian, I guessed. I had wanted to know, I really had. I reminded myself of this. I also reminded myself that I am only half-breed. Not even.

While fully aware how I shall forever and profoundly treasure the experience, I surprisingly disembarked from the cruise with the relief and satisfaction of a teen on the last day of school. As Michael Arlen stated on his first pilgrimage to Armenia, "I saw what I saw and I found what I found." I now truly understood that not feeling a part of the scene I had glimpsed—not growing up within the culture—was all part of the story yet to unfold. My part, as unchangeable as that of my ancestors. I left the ship with a treasure trove of books and histories to guide me beyond those I had devoured to date: works by Peter Balakian, Carol Edgarian, and other contemporary authors, all of whom had eloquently explored themes of Armenian heritage before me, and whose works have sustained my passion. Adding basic history and details that my newly acquired library offered, research now began in earnest. I visited every accessible living relative, each of whom contributed flashes of memory and anecdote that both perpetuated and built on impressions and offered clues from which to dig for further detail.

Meanwhile, I continued to absorb history and began to realize something: the Armenian story is repeatedly mirrored throughout the ages. The Armenian Plateau of Anatolia served as a battlefield since thousands of years B.C., the population decimated over and over again by Roman, Persian, Byzantine, Mongol, and Marmaluke conquering entities long before the Ottoman period. True, Armenia did enjoy a long period of autonomous glory ruled by fierce princes before, and for centuries after, its conversion to Christianity in 301 A.D. The Apostolic version of Armenian Christianity, different from Eastern Orthodox, was fiercely clung to and guarded by the Armenian people. Had they accepted a conversion to Byzantine Orthodoxy that Constantinople tried to exert, power and peace might have prevailed, at least until the Ottoman replacement of Byzantine control.

Discovering how strong and unbreakable the Apostolic Church has remained, one is even more struck by the uniqueness of Kessab with its homogenized blend of three co-existing branches of Christianity: Apostolic, Catholic, and Evangelical. The latter influence is due to a Reform Presbyterian Church mission movement in the Ottoman Empire of the 19th century, especially in Syria. I always marveled that my Christian grandfather migrated to the U.S. from Syria as a Presbyterian! This curiosity finally led me to the missionary movement and, to its credit, the revelation of Armenian dedication to girls' education. Missionaries in Kessab, since the 1850s, profoundly impacted the Karamardian family history— from educating my ancestors to saving lives from immediate danger. Thinking of this, I wanted to begin with the mysteries surrounding the two established family "victims": my great aunts, Mary and Martha.

I was ready to begin in earnest. Now in my late fifties, I cut back on the B&B season and size of my voice studio to make room for travel. It was a decade and a half since Stepan had tragically died on a dance floor, in the arms of his wife. I was left with the single memory from when we met in 1977. I had assumed that my aunts' stories were waiting to be revealed in one specific Armenian diary—Louisa's journal—that her son had dangled at me. The promise of it had sustained me from youth all through my middle years. I could not wait to devour it, but I hesitated to ask for many years, unsure how to appropriately do so.

During one of several trips to visit the Los Angeles cousins, I finally made contact with Seta, Stepan's widow, living on a winery in Gilroy, CA with her new husband. I spoke with her by telephone. Eventually I would visit and interview her, capturing strains of both Louisa and Stepan's stories, but in that first phone call, she gave me the news.

"Oh, Denice! I'm so sad, so heartbroken. Stepan's personal things and papers were all stored in my daughter's basement when it was flooded. My son-in-law had to throw everything out, and the diary is lost!"

My wait was over. The diary had filled my head with obsession. Decades of imagining the actual details of slavery, murder, rescue, and redemption pouring from the pages of Louisa's diary came to an end; a door unequivocally closed. In spite of my disappointment, I surprised myself in that I accepted it immediately. I knew only that Jido's cousin Asadour (Louisa's husband) was involved in the deliverance of both sisters; now, I knew that key to the puzzle was lost. This sense of closure actually delivered new energy and determination to move forward. With not yet a single clue to Mary's story, I was armed with just two paragraphs of Martha's, written to my father. A place to begin. Next stop—Detroit.

I'd heard all about Detroit and the great migration of immigrants who flocked there to work for Ford, but I had always wondered how my great aunts ended up there. The most intriguing stories from the family were that our great aunts had been sex slaves.

The words "Turkish harem" were usually used, and I doubted it was accurate. Exaggeration was a relished skill in my family, so I took nothing for granted. Yet the story consistently concluded with my grandfather and great uncles pooling money to buy their sisters from Turks and bring them to this country. Since we lived in New York, it seemed odd to me that the aunts lived in Michigan but, as a child, I didn't yet know that all three brothers had been living in Detroit at the time. Archie had gone first, upon his arrival to the new world, and kept his last name, Karamardian. He was followed by Leo and Joe and Helen in 1913. The Simon family also migrated there, as did cousin Asadour. This is all documented in the first clues I found. The draft registration cards of 1917.

In Detroit, my cousin Ilene hosted me and provided access to everyone in the family, running me around to interview Martha's descendants and holding family dinners at which I furiously scribbled notes and tried to keep them organized by speaker. What came to me there was a flurry of impressions from a crowd of cousins I was meeting for the first time and who were, curiously, all male. (Ilene was the only granddaughter of Martha's seven grandchildren).

Ilene got right to it. "Can you even imagine what kind of violence—rape, or who knows what—Martha must have endured on that cart journey to the slave camp and then worse at the slave camp? She was never right after that!" And she pointed out, "She had a loving husband who treated her so tenderly and devoted children. Yet still she spent her life in and out of mental wards, unable to recover. What must have happened to damage her so badly!"

I possessed the few paragraphs offered up by Martha, revealing a brief, but real first day of a life that no fourteen-year-old girl should even imagine, let alone live through over the span of four years. The paragraphs scream silent words, too, the unsaid portion of her story, the part that fills Ilene's head, after the cart rumbled away with a girl in shock. Five blank years of unknown trauma, until Martha arrived at Joe and Helen's home in Port Huron.

My cousins in Detroit shared a favorite story: that Martha's brothers had met Gazar Karagozian (their grandfather) in a shoe shop, and told him, "Our sister comes next week. Meet us back here on Friday. We will bring her." It was not necessarily an arranged marriage, yet I can't help but wonder: what choice might nineteen-year-old Martha—accustomed only to slavery since the age of fourteen—have felt at the time?

How did women absorb trauma one hundred years ago? I ask myself that constantly. Processing trauma is such a tenuous, fickle concept. It occurs to me that I don't even know how I have processed trauma of my own, as I attempt to consider the teeny tiny glimpse into lives of my ancestors through second and thirdhand knowledge or a document here and there, devoid of emotional clues. Words never spoken, not even uttered among themselves. Certainly not by strong, stoic Mary (or so my imagination decides). What of frail Martha, who never overcame her memories? Clearly, her secrets stuck to her, like an infected scar that scabs over from time to time but refuses to heal permanently. How did her demons torment, to the point that even her loving husband could not sustain her? If I did have clues, even written ones, might they be subject to misconstrued meaning and innuendo, even misinformation? It was simply not meant to be clear. Wait! I imagine that I hear Mary Karamardian Simon whisper...

"Sometimes the story is to stay alive."

Which brings me to Mary—no interview, no written story, no information. The genocide affected our family towns in the summer of 1915, the march from Kessab in August of that year. But Mary's first son was born in 1915, indicating she was safely in Detroit before the war. Confirming with her own descendants that she was indeed taken a slave, I had to reconstruct her journey somehow. Something Ilene's mother, Colleen (Martha's daughter-in-law) said often and emphatically, ran over and over in my mind.

"Mary was always so proud of her arranged marriage. She spoke often of how she appreciated it and that nowadays people didn't know how to make marriage work."

The statement lingered with a teasing importance. I already held the mystery of a lost brother in my mental files. This bit of information led directly to another mystery. How could it be that an Armenian girl would have entered into an arranged marriage with a Syrian man? This just didn't make sense. "Married off" to an Arab! The more I learned about Armenian culture, the more mysterious Mary's marriage seemed. After years of pondering the anomaly, it occurred to me that just maybe, the fact that the marriage was arranged is the key to the rest of the mystery surrounding Mary. There must be more to it, some connection.

Aunt Susie and Aunt Laura both described their Aunt Mary as a no-nonsense, strict, and unemotional person. This contrasted starkly with the seemingly warm-hearted Martha who was, however, so fragile and mentally vulnerable. The personality differences between the two sisters intrigued me, reminding me of the character contrast between their nieces, Susie and Laura. The push and pull of opposite personalities, the differences in age and experience with a line of brothers between them—these parallels blow my mind sometimes. The elder aunt sisters had spent all of their childhoods together in Latakia; one the female head of household; the other, the baby of a family. In America, it seems, they spent every day together in Martha's kitchen, cooking and chatting about who knows what?

"Mary lived upstairs in the same house and kept it immaculate. They cooked all day in Martha's kitchen. Mary took her meals home without ever having messed her spotless kitchen," said Ilene.

Evidently, that kitchen hosted many a young Armenian wife, newly arrived in their new world. Two such women, Sarah Churukian and Armine Tomassian, described to me their introductions to the new country in the warmth and camaraderie of Martha's Detroit kitchen with Mary, Martha, and two Aunt Alices. I like to imagine that kitchen as a gathering spot, a women's world like the shoe shops and card tables that provided social environments for the men of my family.

I grew obsessed with the mystery of Mary's ordeal and life. Everyone confirmed that she had been taken as a slave but, I reasoned, her story must be different—a prelude to the troubles yet to come to the family left helplessly behind in wartime to face the century's first genocide about to rain down on them. I could find no record of Mary Karamardian (except for a marriage certificate which identified her as Mary Peter). So I repeatedly turned to that instinctual dilemma: what was the connection between Ameen Simon and Mary's brothers that would lead to an arranged marriage between their Armenian sister and a Syrian?

I reminded myself that my Armenian grandfather also chose to marry an Arab, and this was a time when Armenians were poison to many Arabs, as some had been persecuted by Turks for helping or protecting Armenians. Everyone knew tensions were strong between them from the stories of Sito's villagers forbidding her near my Jido, and how hand-to-hand combat had settled the matter. There HAD to be a connection. Gratefully, there exists a large paper trail of Ameen's family. His father's name, John Simon, is one of the most common names on record. But when I happened upon a passport application for John Simon of Detroit, I struck gold. This John Simon had once lived in Myers, NY! The glaringly obvious common denominator had to be the salt block—which led to the next puzzle.

What would draw a Muslim family to a small upstate New York village, largely settled by Syrian Christians? Nothing. So, what if, I mused, the "alleged" conversion to Christianity took place in Syria? That would motivate a family to emigrate in the early 1900s. Again, a mic drop: the 1910 census from Myers, NY informs that the Simon family were all born in Latakia! If they had converted there, it could have been by missionaries. No matter how long they had been Christian, surely the boys might have attended the mission school in Latakia? The plot thickened further when I noted on the same census that John Simon was an 'instructor' at the salt block. This could only mean he already spoke English and the only individuals in Syria teaching English at the time were missionaries. At this point, nothing could keep me from fantasizing the possibility that the Simon and Karamardian families were acquainted in Latakia—a longshot, true, but I was emboldened with a newfound confidence in my "imagination."

When I asked Aunt Laura, did she remember her Uncle Ameen coming to the farm with Aunt Mary and the cousins, she said she didn't think so; she could barely picture him. And she pointed out, "Ma didn't like Ameen." When I asked why, "Well, I always assumed 'cause he was Muslim!"

Well, he wasn't. I can imagine that Ameen did not have the luxury of extended vacation time from Ford to take a train to upstate New York with his wife and kids in summers. After discovering his father was an instructor, it occurred to me that Ameen was likely educated, and that my illiterate, earthy, raw, farming grandmother may well have felt self-conscious and inferior around the Simons. As devout as she was, and just as opinionated, her children may have made certain assumptions about her prejudices. How odd, how sad really, if the insecurities of one person can be misinterpreted by a whole generation and could perpetuate unless someone or something comes along to bust the myth that has settled into the unintended result. I am fairly certain that my grandmother's attitude towards her brother-in-law serves as an example of this danger.

Gratefully, I finally met some of Mary's offspring—the four daughters of her first born, Albert. I joined the sisters for lunch at the Delray Beach home of the eldest, Laurie. I struggled to absorb all I could take in during two short hours that sped by, thrilled by these other—new and different—experiences of the ancestors. A fresh new vision of Mary unfolded before me. Unlike my aunts, who had feared their Aunt Mary, these sisters remembered a kind, loving grandmother who waited for them at the top of a staircase with wide open arms and folded them into warm embraces. I specifically asked about religion, not expecting an answer, while explaining my confusion about the arranged marriage.

Amazingly, Laurie told me, "I remember a story about my grandfather, Ameen, being given a Bible by his father when he left for America, half of it translated to Arabic. His father told him he would need it, as he would only find Bibles in English there…"

So. That settled it. The Simon family was Christian back in Latakia, and for how long who can know! Ameen had emigrated first, maybe before my grandfather. The children would have likely attended the mission school there—the same one Jido and his siblings attended. I laughed to myself. The Simons were more involved in their faith than the Peters! A string of myths that had endured lifetimes now, and at last, dissolved. I embraced an entirely new vision of the Simons, especially when Laurie followed with an afterthought.

"And someone in the family was a missionary…."

CHAPTER 12

SISTERS

Los Angeles - 1947

LAURA

Laura settled onto the bench of the train car, clutching a cigar box on her lap, and waved to her father on the platform. The train lurched in the initial second that it pulled out of Ithaca's Lehigh Station, then settled into a smooth crawl. The first thing she saw was Abbott's store before the view out the window yielded to the marshy flats that dominated the valley it snaked through. Hills rising from both sides sported grey bark tree trunks and leafless branches like bleakly plastered stripes against the white flooring of partial snow covering. Laura would soon pass out of the State of New York for the first time in her life. She would cross the entire breadth of the United States to attend her sister's wedding.

By the time the shadows lengthened to dusk, the gentle hills had given way to the flat emptiness of the country Laura knew from school geography to be the Midwest. At first light she awoke to the endless horizon of Iowa, then Kansas. She had closed her eyes and slept sitting without ever releasing her hold on the cardboard box in her lap. Fingering her precious cargo—the pile of postcards sent from faraway places—Laura was now able to imagine her brothers crisscrossing the country on these very tracks, to and from furloughs and trips home. In some cases, there were journeys to reunite with—even propose to—beloveds, as in the case of George and Gloria, or to hurriedly marry, as in the case of Jake and Hazel. Remembering, she smiled and peeked inside the box as if she was checking on those places the brothers had inhabited or visited—that they hadn't disappeared on her.

She carried the box to share with her big sister, who no doubt also deserved to experience the wonder of their brothers' lives during the war. It did not occur to her to question Susie's interest in the paragraphs scrawled on the flip side of photos from one state or another. The cards had provided the basic sustenance of at least four long winters and summers for Laura and her parents, representing not only all her brothers' war lives, but all that they at home had endured waiting. Laura also carried the new *Vanity Fair* magazine she had bought on payday that week and opening it now, she flipped through the pages for a moment. She set it aside, though, as she distractedly found herself drawn mostly to reliving highlights of the military lives of brothers. Opening the box, she picked up a card with a picture of the Grand Canyon on its cover side—from brother Ark.

George's transformation was the most remarkable, or at least the most demonstrated, since Ark turned out to be the most prolific letter writer. His march from love at first sight on a blind date with Gloria to his state of mind when he wrote the card from Williams Airfield after his transfer there, was especially romantic. George wrote how difficult it was to focus on his work for an entire day, and the relief he felt each night just to be able to stop and think about her and write about her and dream about her! Wasn't it great that he had just bought the South Danby farm from their parents; he and Gloria were trying to make a go at raising chickens while George worked days as an electrician. And Gloria was pregnant! Laura, Joe, and Helen moved to the old farmhouse on King Road which they had left for South Danby before Laura was born. After renting for some twenty years, the old farm presented quite a mess to overcome. Life at home seemed to have shifted into a new gear since the war.

Susie had begun to write to her too, now that she was living so far away in California, and a friendship between the sisters was building in the way Laura had craved for in her teens. Her big sister was her hero. After graduation from nursing school, Susie and a girlfriend took a driving vacation all the way out west—such courage Laura could not imagine. Susie immediately got a job at a Los Angeles hospital with her new status and skills. Aunty Satinique invited Susie to stay with her and Uncle Archie, which seemed awful generous since they had just had George and Gloria with them for some time.

Susie wrote that Aunty Satinique was secretly plotting marriage for her to her oldest son Avedis (who the family calls Eddie). Satinique had come to America, a survivor and a widow with two sons from her first marriage, and had a third son, Nishan, after Uncle Archie married her. However, Susie, ever the perfect rebel, fell for the younger son, Horon, and they had been sneaking out away from the family eyes to be together. Laura just loved the intimate details of a secret love affair, and the sense of danger it held, from dramatic letters that far surpassed women's magazines like the one on her lap. Now she was on her way to Los Angeles, California to stand witness for her big sister!

The girls' youngest brothers, Sam and Moosey were also in California and would be attending the Valentine's Day wedding. After the war, those two—restless as ever—decided to try their fortunes in the state that had so impressed Sam while he was stationed there. Moosey was just plain bored with Ithaca after the excitement of war and was game for something different. Laura's anticipation of adventure so far from home with three of her siblings was enhanced with the bonus of spending time with Uncle Archie, Auntie, and cousin Nishan, none of whom she'd seen since before the war. The best part, though, was the sizzle of being part of the bride's wedding plans!

Susie was admittedly different from the rest of her family, a little bossy perhaps, yet more sophisticated and worldly. Anticipating all that was to come, Laura wished her parents were on the train with her, about to reunite with her father's brother and family and witness their first daughter wed. Were Helen not feeling poorly and rather weak lately, Laura wondered if they would have considered it. They may still have seen such a trip as a frivolity, but she wasn't sure. Regardless, her mother seemed much too fragile for any discussion of travel.

The mountains were a relief to behold, even when the tracks appeared harrowing— close to rock walls or drop off ledges—and seemed to make the trip worth the monotony that prevailed in the first day, like a reward for staying on board through the flat parts. In this, her first time away from New York State, Laura realized that she was quite attached to its natural and gentle landscape, especially the hills, trees, and gullies. But neither was she disappointed with the glamour of Los Angeles, proudly shared by a big chunk of her family.

There were Sam and Moosey, Uncle Archie's tribe of five and Aunty Satinique's extended family of siblings, Susie… and surprise—for the first time, Laura got to meet Uncle Leo. It happened at the flower shop at 59th Street that Uncle Archie owned! From the descriptions she had heard for years from her mother and sister, she was mighty surprised by his charm and hospitality. He enjoyed showing off the sights of the city. In turn, Laura enjoyed the opportunity, while everyone gathered around after supper one night, to read to the family from some of her brothers' postcards—all this met with belly laughs at the things the boys had written while suffering stress and homesickness. Naturally, Sam and Moosey made a big deal of picking on and laughing at each other.

Laura especially cherished the 'sister time' alone with Susie; shopping, preparing for the wedding, painting fingernails for her very first time, and girly chit chat that was non-existent at home on the South Danby farm. In fact, this was sisterly life the two had never enjoyed, due to the ten years in age that separated them. She told Susie about the boy she had been seeing, but who had just broken it off because she couldn't go out on Saturday nights. He suspected she was cheating. His name was Nick Bellisario—the first boy she ever dated.

"What the hell is wrong with you? Why don't you go out on Saturday?" demanded Susie.

"Because... well, I don't want anyone coming to the house to pick me up. Can you imagine Pa meeting a beau? I can't even!" Laura began with a stammer and ended in a defensive yell, but the two girls dissolved into giggles, and then tears, from laughing so hard.

"Laura, listen to me! What you gotta do is find an apartment downtown with some girlfriends. You need to learn some independence, or you won't even know how to talk with a boy—let alone a husband. You sure don't want to be married off like our aunts, do you?"

CHAPTER 13

Ithaca - 1948

JOE

When a large property at the corner of King and Danby Roads came up for sale—a house, cabins, a shower house, and acreage on all four corners, including the old schoolhouse—the move to the new, smaller house at 105 King Road was completed. The old farmhouse at the top of King Road rented up again for $25 a month; this helped fill the money gap now that Joe had both retired from the plant and no longer owned a milk herd. It seemed like the "Peter herd" was thinning out too, or rather spreading out. Joe and Helen's sons were all nearby. And finally, two grandsons were added to the tribe in '47. Charlotte and John welcomed "Joey" in January and Gloria gave birth to Michael in July. Helen was over the moon. The same summer, Sam and Moosey made their way home from California, but not without drama.

Sam's '27 Chrysler may have made it to California, but on the way home they only almost reached Gallup, New Mexico, when the car announced its death, much like the old farm horse Dolly back in the early '30s. The rusty radiator exploded wide open. The boys considered casting about for a junkyard but realized that the frame was too rusted to attach another radiator. Too broke to afford train fare or repairs, they left the car where it died and hitchhiked across the Rockies and the plains.

Joe gave them the southwest corner chunk of the property at King and Danby Roads, on which the brothers opened up a Gulf gas station. They lived in an apartment upstairs for a year or so, until Moosey got married and kicked Sam out. Moosey had always been sweet on a South Danby neighbor—Fred Hill's daughter, Lois. They would marry in 1950. But meanwhile, and even while settling down, the youngest son found an outlet for his nervous energy and need for action. The two brothers immersed themselves in the stock car circuit, combining their love of tinkering with engines and the thrill of the racing scene.

Driving car numbers 99 and 101, Sam and Moses Peter became known as the "Terrors of Ithaca." Their mother hated their racing habit and refused to hear about it. Not only did she clamp her lips and discourage the sharing of racing news, the subject became forbidden to mention in the house. Finally, however, their father was cajoled into attending just one race—a disastrous experience for a man who had spent four years waiting out the war while praying for the safety of his sons. During the race, Moosey miscalculated his speed and angle on a sharp turn. The car flipped—not an uncommon event for the racers—causing its battery to come loose and roll down the track. Joe

Peter thought he was seeing his son's head rolling and flew out onto the track himself, screaming, "Mussa, Mussa, my son!" There was no consoling him. Although Moosey crawled out from the car frame unhurt, Joe couldn't take it again.

Sam decided to cash in on his radio and mechanical abilities. He built a TV and appliance store on the opposite east corner of the intersection, and began his own business, while Moosey and Lois expanded the service station to include a little grocery. Sam brought a little black and white, tiny box television over to his mother as a surprise gift. Helen was fatigued often in those days and napped in the afternoons. But somehow, the late Saturday night wrestling show on the television captured her imagination and she made a point to wake up and watch the sport, to the point of obsession. Her sons couldn't help but tease her.

"Ma, you know it's all rigged, don't cha?"

"Don't tell me nuttin! I don't wanna know tat!"

Late in summer of 1949, George pulled into the drive just as Joe was taking a batch of his round Syrian loaves out of the oven. Now in retirement, he baked regularly and kept all his tribe supplied in fresh bread.

"Pa, we got a call, a message from Binghamton came to the farm! You're gonna have a visitor tomorrow. From the old country!"

Joe and Helen got up early and drove out to the farm the next morning, a Saturday. He wanted to be there before the arrival of who knew? They were rewarded with hugs from their two-year-old grandson. There was no exact time to be expecting the mystery visitors from Syria, so Joe took out the tractor to warm up for George and put little Michael in front of him, driving around in circles until satisfied with the boy's constant giggles. Then, a little tired, he settled onto a porch rocker and waited, while Gloria and Helen took Michael inside to bathe. George was out in the tractor cutting down hay, so when the car pulled up, Joe was alone on the porch. He didn't know the young couple that emerged from the Buick, nor what connection was about to be revealed, only that the call had come from his cousin Sammy in Binghamton. Anticipation suddenly surged through his blood and a spontaneous smile broke a crack into his face. They were of Kessab, after all. The young woman spoke first.

"Hovsep? Hovsep Karamardian? Mr. Peter?" tentatively, she didn't know what to call him, having been advised of the name change, "I am Armine, daughter of Boghos."

Ah, cousin Boghos! Son of Joe's Aunt Mary Boghossian. He had returned to Kessab—with Asadour—they'd gone back to fight the war together. This was meant to be a short visit. Armine and her husband planned to stop in Rochester for the night and then on to Detroit where they would visit with Marta and Mary and cousin Alice. Ultimately, the young couple would settle in Los Angeles and Joe told them, "Ask Marta for Khatchig's address in Los Angeles." He couldn't then know how warmly they would be inducted to the area by Archie and Leo. But as of now, they had only been twenty-four hours in the United States and Joe imagined he could smell the mountains of Kessab on their clothes. Fantasy of an old man, he thought.

The couple described their journey that began with the local taxi ride by Misak Boghossian's three mail horses to Antwerp, then and on to Greece and Marseille, and following the most common ship journey to New York. In Binghamton, they visited with relatives Abe Boghossian and the Giragossians. Joe introduced Armine and Diran to Helen, who had emerged from inside the house during the telling. Then he asked the question that was burning him with impatience: what news of his cousin Asadour?

"Oh, dear. You do not know, then..." Armine hesitated and glanced at her new husband for guidance. She felt the breeze cradle her face, licking it like a loving puppy might, and she tried to organize her thoughts.

"Asadour died—pneumonia they said, or tuberculosis. But it seemed like the sickness of the little ones before him—typhoid, that is according to Louisa." Armine sensed the impact of her words on this distant uncle and slowed down her speech, in deference both to his need to absorb the old information that was new to him, and perhaps his distance from the Kessabtsi dialect. They had warned her that he navigated his life in Arabic, due to his Syrian wife.

"It was before the new war. Sadly, Louisa was in a bad way without him and two sons to support."

"Two sons?" Joe had heard that only one of three boys had survived.

"Yes, Manas and Stepan, an intelligent boy!" Armine realized that this too was news. "The fourth son was about seven when Asadour died. But Stepan is an academic wonder and is the pride of the American missionaries. Louisa now works for the missionaries in Latakia."

After tea, Diran and Armine drove the car back down Peter Road to South Danby where they would turn northward toward Ithaca and Rochester. Joe wondered if he would ever meet them again and found himself lost in reflection and memory for the remainder of the day—a condition he was not comfortable with and typically avoided at all cost. However, vignettes floated around his brain like balloons as he relived Asadour's panic to get back to the first war and his Louisa, his teaming up with Boghos to fight with the French; later, Asadour's letters and aid in helping his sisters through the worst of their ordeals—scenes he was mercifully spared from in his blissful ignorance. What an angel his cousin had been for them all. How little he had done in return for those who remained. Could he have helped? He didn't know how.

But when his thoughts moved on to another Asadour—his brother—missing somewhere in the southern hemisphere, Joe knew it was time to switch off his mind before he plunged into a bottomless pit that went nowhere. Back at the little house on King Road, Joe baked some pastries and bread, filling the house with aromas, and Helen napped before her wrestling show. It was Saturday, after all.

Two weeks after Mose and Lois' wedding in 1950, a telegram arrived at the farm from Detroit. George rushed over to King Road to read it to his parents. It was Martha who sent the wire, on behalf of Mary. Mary's husband Ameen Simon had been very ill for some time in a hospital, after recovering from surgery. On

March 25th, he stepped out of a high floor hospital window to his death. The circumstances were murky: the hospital, while suggesting suicide, remained silent about the clear possibility of hallucinations from the drugs given him. Martha begged Joe to come. Mitch drove him out via the fastest route, cutting through Canada from north of Buffalo, at the big falls. Joe had forgotten to bring his citizenship papers but thankfully, was let through, which amazed him.

It was a good week that he spent with his sisters, though Joe was somewhat surprised how stoic Mary remained through the arrangements. She did not believe her husband had taken his own life—in fact, few did. There was little cooperation from either the hospital or the police and Mary appeared stiff and weary with the responsibility of maintaining normal appearances. Her eldest son, Albert, supported her and remained at her side throughout. All four sons were mostly settled; Mary was already blessed with a granddaughter, and anxious for more.

Martha was more emotional than the grieving widow but managed to graciously host her brother and nephew. Joe delighted to meet his niece Chi Chi's husband, Harry Karagosian, who, like his own Moses and Martha's Hagop, had fought in the Battle of the Bulge. But Harry had been taken prisoner in a place he called 'Neubrandenburg, Mecklenburg.' Joe didn't even try to pronounce the name in his head as he listened to Harry describe his ordeal. He'd been shot in the ankle by a fourteen-year-old German and could not escape. Once captured, he was moved around between four different prison camps and was grateful to have survived. Whether from ignorance or innocence, Joe silently allowed himself to indulge in some relief, in the thought that his son had liberated such a camp, rather than suffer in one.

The younger Harry—Martha's last child—was working as a musician with the Detroit Symphony and Joe was puzzled by his parents' rejection of the choice. Gazar expressed disdain at a profession he did not consider respectable and simply refused to honor his son's talent. Joe asked his sister about it.

"But Hovsep-jan, how will he support a family, playing on a flute every night?" Joe shook his head in wonder but didn't argue. Even he knew the instrument was a clarinet, not a flute.

In the spring, Laura moved to downtown Ithaca with two girlfriends. Joe knew she enjoyed her new freedom outside of work. The bank opened on Saturday mornings for a half day. Every single Saturday at noon, he made a point to be waiting outside to bring her home for the weekend and take her back to work on Monday morning. He did this for Helen, more than for himself, who cooked all day Saturday to feed this last child—the only child she still had any grip or influence on. Joe suspected that Laura turned down dates for Saturday night. Sam and Mose hinted as much. He didn't care. She was the last. He would cling as long as possible.

But his little girl did get to take a trip to Philadelphia with her mother and Sam. Sam drove them down in his brand-new car to attend a wedding of Satinique's nephew. Satinique would be there, of course, but Archie could not leave his flower shop to make the trip from California. So Joe declined to go as well.

Laura was introduced to a brother of this nephew groom—an occasion carefully planned by Satinique herself—and hope sprung that she might date this Harry Basjian. After the wedding, they added another day to the trip and drove to Atlantic City. Joe listened to the story upon their return, Laura still giggling as if it had just happened.

Strolling down the pier while looking for a spot for Helen to sit and rest, Laura stopped short and gasped. She pointed frantically, unable to find the words for at least a full minute. While she mimed and pointed and choked, Helen and Sam tried to follow her gaze, shaking their heads.

"Ma! Sam! It's Frank Sinatra!" Laura was even more aghast when she recognized the woman accompanying him—the famous Ava Gardner. The scandal was grand, since Sinatra was married at the time, and Laura spoke of nothing else for weeks afterward. To Joe's amazement, Helen continued to laugh whenever it was brought up. But he was distracted with his own elation. The match with Harry Basjian, an Armenian connected to family through his sister-in-law Satinique, was even recommended by his brother. The relief he felt for his youngest daughter was real and exhilarating. By God, he thought, both my daughters marrying back into the Armenian fold… well that will more than make up for a string of American daughters-in-law. Then he laughed at himself, partly in amazement that he should care about such a thing by this point.

By 1953 there were eleven grandchildren regularly visiting the house and the couple were content to delight at the growing brood. Their lives were full with family, Joe's baking, and Helen's TV wrestling show. They attended *hufflas* in Myers and Geneva, *mahrajans* in Syracuse, and visited family regularly. The year kicked off in January with the arrival of the letter.

It came from the West Indies, the Caribbean island of Dominica. Joe was beside himself, his heart flying instantly to his dear brother Asadour, seen last in 1908. Laura opened it and smoothed out the creases. The handwriting was rough and barely legible.

"Dear Mrs. Peter, I know your sister and she is wanting to come to America. Please send $100.00 for her passage. You can send to this place on the envelope. A friend."

Laura's jaw didn't close after she finished reading and looked up into her mother's face, which was… was it white? Ashen? With all the stories told about Melkia throughout her life, no one had ever heard mention of a sister. Neither from Helen nor Moses, her brother.

"Ma, what is this?" Helen did not speak. She gazed in front of her, like a deer caught in headlights—thinking. No one spoke, not even Joe who curiously watched his wife.

Finally she said, "Yes, I have a sister. She left the village before me. Disgraced. Never heard from her."

"What is her name, Ma?" It took a long time for Helen to answer the question.

"Najwa." Then, as if she remembered something, "Did they say her name?"

"No, Ma, no mention of her name. Could this be true? Would she be in this… Dominica?"

"How can I know? She just… disappeared. We were told not to say her name again."

Joe then explained the scam systems he had witnessed in the Caribbean—the extortion of relatives for money. By now these would be more sophisticated, but the gist still the same: a so-called friend pretends to speak for your relative. The lack of a name clinched it for him.

"If we send ta money, you can bet we not gonna see any Najwa."

Perhaps the subject would not have died, except that Helen took ill again. Joe prayed as hard as he had after Laura's birth twenty-five years earlier, when he took his wife, bleeding and in pain, back to hospital.

CHAPTER 14

Goodbyes

Ithaca – 1953

Susie et al

The train ride across country with two little ones was a challenge, even for a gritty woman like Susie. She hated leaving Horon, the sweetest man she could have ever hoped for. Her brothers teased her every chance they got, saying her marriage would work only because she chose a man who would do her bidding. Little did they know the truth of the balance she and Horon had found in each other, and a friendship beyond any she had ever dreamed. She was going to miss her confidant while navigating the murky waters of life back home with the family she had escaped from—but was in the process of discovering she still loved fiercely.

Squeals and clangs of train metal components were constant. The train came to stops regularly, several per state, as it chugged its way across the plains. Also constant was Stephen's dialogue, typical perhaps of any curious four-year-old. But Susie wearied of it, while two-year-old Larry made squirming his three-day occupation. She was grateful when they fell silent for the five minutes or so it took them to eat a meal, and she could turn her attention to the landscape passing by, if only momentarily.

She remembered, however, the panic she had felt eight years earlier on her drive west with Arlene—panic not at the adventure ahead, but at the flat landscape and miles upon miles of rows of low-growing corn stalks. For Susie, as for her father and sister, the lack of gentle hills, when they gave way to endless landscape stretched out before her, left her bereft. Her anxiety was based on a sense of going nowhere, no physical curve or visible break to eternity. What a relief it was, to cross the Ohio line into Pennsylvania and the low-rising hills of southern New York. The landscape of home seemed to offer nurturing promise, in spite of the reality she had experienced in home life.

The last time she'd been home, just before her California journey after graduation, Jake and Hazel were living in the farmhouse, too. They had not yet bought the house in downtown Ithaca. She had felt uneasy around Hazel, who had her own ways and customs and kept to herself. Hazel represented what Susie aspired to as a nurse, even while she remained holed up alone in her room. For a brief moment, Susie now allowed herself to reflect on how lost Hazel may have felt thrown into that ridiculous household of wild men. But at the time she, herself, had been so exhilarated to leave that life behind and, with a hardened heart, drive toward her future.

This was the first return home, a triumphant return, and she approached it with pride. Now a big shot at her hospital, she was in charge of the nurses on her hospital ward. It was a good and highly respected job. And she had two grandsons to present to her parents, adding to the growing third generation. There was nothing to be ashamed of or to shirk from. In fact, she had accomplished as much as any of them, she thought to herself. What mattered anyway, the force that brought her all the way from Los Angeles back to Ithaca, was to care for her mother. It was the chance to "be" what she had vowed to become the last time she watched her mother rushed off to the hospital.

The small house on King Road was a big adjustment from the old South Danby farmhouse that George and Gloria had taken over and since sold. No longer did Joe and Helen wield unlimited space for whomever may appear at any time, day or night. Laura had moved downtown with girlfriends but still came home on weekends. She had written to Susie about more than that, too. It seems Laura decided not to be pushed into marriage and wrote to break it off with Harry Basjian. Susie was actually surprised at her courage—proud, too. She had expected their Pa to be disappointed but was shocked at just how furious he was with Laura. What a new development for the "can do no wrong Zaha," thought Susie, wondering where the subject stood now.

The train pulled into the Lehigh Station at midnight. She was moved to see her father waiting by the platform. He helped support a sleepy Stephen, who half stumbled to the car while an immobile Larry was draped over Joe's shoulder, never opening his eyes. Susie followed with suitcases and, too tired for conversation, fell asleep as soon as she hit the bed in Laura's room. First thing in the morning, Lois Hill (now Lois Peter) crossed the street and took both boys in hand, assuring Susie from over her shoulder that they'd have a grand old time. Joe and Susie left immediately for the hospital. They found Helen sedated and groggy. But when she opened her eyes she smiled to her eldest daughter, sending a rush of warm feelings through Susie's torso. Susie tried to recall if she'd seen her mother smile at her in the past, which turned her giddiness to worry. What was wrong?

Helen underwent the second half of the hysterectomy that had been performed on her in 1933. Now, twenty years later, Susie knew the procedure was no longer split into two parts. In fact, Susie possessed a whole lot of cutting-edge medicinal knowledge and had to bite her tongue to maintain professional respect on more than one frustrating encounter with doctors from this "hillbilly" (in her opinion) town. Although Hazel worked at the hospital, she was on another ward, so neither woman was in charge of decisions surrounding Helen's care. Yet soon enough, Susie would perform the role she had envisioned the last time she had stood by a bed in this very hospital, when they had taken Helen home in her care—she, a mere teenager. Susie suspected something and asked the doctor to see the X-ray. Cancer had spread to the stomach. She would not leave her mother's side again.

On June 11th, available family gathered to celebrate two milestones: Laura's birthday and George and Gloria's anniversary. Laura was excited throughout her workday, counting the minutes until Pa would pick her up. The girls at work treated her at lunchtime, which helped distract her, but she ached for the closeness of her family surrounding a dinner table—a scene so sorely missed during the war years without any of them.

Susie and Joe prepared dinner for the occasion with Helen sitting up on the living room settee, interjecting with bursts of energy that sometimes came upon her. Joe also made Laura's favorite meat pies—lahmajoun. After the meal, the group remained seated around the table to savor the round cake with white, almond frosting. Mitch, his mother-in-law, Helen, Mitch's wife Pat, little Mitchy, a pregnant Gloria, Susie, little Stephen, Lois, Moosey, George, little Michael, and Joe sang together to Laura, now twenty-five years old and beaming as she stood by her cake. They sang to George and Gloria, now eight years married and with 2.6 children. Off in Laura's bedroom, Lois' mother watched over three more sleeping children. Conversation turned to the letter, and for the first time, the Peter boys heard of the mysterious aunt on a Caribbean island—supposedly.

"What do you think, Mitch?" asked Helen, after a confusing five minutes of garbled overlapping voices from everybody talking at once.

"A scam, Ma! No question about it," said Mitch, and everyone else agreed.

"But what if it's not?" demanded Laura, who was thinking fast. How on earth would they have been found, if there was no seed of truth to it? Where could the person have come upon information about Ma? In a typical reaction to Laura's venturing an opinion, her brothers all laughed—even Susie, and she shrank inside.

"Zaha, that's the point—the scam, the hook! They pick you at random and take a chance. They don't know if you really do have a sister...."

Laura told Susie later that night how odd she found it that none of her siblings were at all curious about the aunt they had just learned about. She couldn't just shake it off. Susie hadn't given it much thought since the subject got cut off so quickly by none other than Helen, herself. Nobody in the household yet appreciated Helen's ability to see an opportunity and jump on it; in that moment, the mother of eight saw her opening and made her bargain.

"I'll tell you what! I'll forget all about the letter and Najwa if Mussa and Sam will promise to forget all about racing the cars!" There was dead silence around the table. Only Mose was on hand to speak for the "Terrors of Ithaca." Sam was off somewhere, at a race presumably. Mose promised his mother he would have the conversation with Sam. No one noticed when Lois smiled to herself.

Later that night, the sisters slept in Laura's room and picked up on the sisterly comfort they had discovered in Los Angeles. Susie couldn't wait to get to the bottom of the 'boy drama' Laura had introduced but not completed. When asked about their father's reaction to her breaking the engagement, Laura surprised her again.

"Yeah, he was hopping mad... but Ma, Susie! You shoulda heard Ma! Right in front of Pa she said, 'Don't you dare marry anyone you don't love!' Pa never said another word about it!"

Then Laura told Susie her new secret. Her pal at the bank, Bob Black, and his wife Alice, set her up on a blind date with

Bob's friend—tall, gangly Bill Smith. Joe still waited for Laura every Saturday at noon to take her home for the weekend. Laura had finally decided she was ready to let a boy come to the house to pick her up. Joe was in the kitchen when Bill arrived, and Helen called, "'Come meet the boy!' But," said Laura, "Pa yells from the kitchen, 'I'm not meeting anymore goddamn men!' so loud Bill could hear him clear as day. I was mortified! Then Ma says real sweet, 'He seems like a nice boy…'" The sisters collapsed in belly laughs as if they were little girls again, and their father banged on the wall and told them to keep it down, which caused them to fly off into more giggles which they attempted to stifle with hands.

"Anyway, Pa actually likes Bill now. Can you guess why? He's a farmer!" More laughs.

The next day, another letter arrived. This one came from California, from Armine Thompson, now settled and writing to share some news. Laura read it to the family:

"Do you remember the boy I spoke of—Asadour and Louisa's boy in Lattakia? Stepan has brought honor to the entire Armenian people! After his diploma from American Missionary School last year, he has now won the Baccalaureate of Holy Earth Lycee—the highest academic award in all of Syria! An Armenian has taken the prize!"

Such a thing had never before happened. Evidently, even the President of Syria was impressed. The letter went on to explain that the President summoned Stepan to Damascus to tutor his children. Stepan was taking his mother, Louisa, and brother, Manasse, to live with him in the Syrian capital.

Armine thanked Joe again for the hospitality and closed with: "My father sent this news to me. How proud your cousin Asadour would be of his son… the Golden Boy of Armenians. I wanted you to know."

"What do you know!" It seemed like Pa couldn't think of anything else to say, as if the thing was incomprehensible to him. But, knowing something of the Armenian community in Los Angeles, Susie knew how big a deal it was.

When the first snows began to swirl and skip on the November winds, and steel grey skies descended on Ithaca, Helen languished—and her children had to make some decisions. Susie, who had hoped to return to her beloved Horon with their sons for Christmas, now understood that if she did so, she would not be seeing her mother again. Perhaps she could persuade Horon to come east if he could get some time off work.

Laura, engaged to her farmer, had hoped for a Christmas wedding—or even a Valentine's one. She decided they'd best put it off a few months, and wait and see. And Sam, too! Sam had gone on a service call to repair a TV for the Newhart family. While there, his attention was drawn to a photo that took his breath away. The wild, elusive Sam Peter fell hard for the Newharts' daughter Ruth before he ever saw her in person. They began dating when the holiday season kicked off. Like Laura, Sam would delay marriage plans because of Helen. But he surprised all of them by how anxious he was to tie the knot.

The family gratefully surrounded Helen throughout the holidays, coming and going and taking instructions from Susie, who held court as Helen's private nurse and caregiver. Grandchildren were paraded around Helen and made her laugh—even shed a tear of laughter at times. She loved to watch the boys: they started off playing in a corner—Michael, Eric, Mitchy, Joey, and Stephen—but four six-year-olds will eventually get too rowdy and be hustled from any room. The little girls were each unique and a few personalities sparked—Vicky, Joanie, Patrice, and the raucous laugh of Lorraine. Toddlers Larry and Christy were kept at bay but allowed to bumble through now and again. Everyone agreed, it was a joyous but subdued season.

The darkness deepened in January. Helen held on for weeks, but weakened daily. Susie sat on her bed one morning, and held Helen's hand tenderly while asking herself, Why have we never done this before? Why does it feel so new to hold my own mother's hand? Just then Helen's eyes flew open and she gazed at her daughter with a love Susie hadn't recognized.

"Can you ever forgive me?" Helen's voice was raspy and weak, yet clear. Susie leaned in to hear better, her face an open question toward her mother. Helen continued, "I treated you poor. You were the oldest. It was the way I knew...."

After Helen fell off to sleep, one of the stories she loved the most to tell around the stove came to Susie's mind. She remembered hearing it at both the farmhouse up the road on King, and the big farm in South Danby, and especially the way in which Helen told it:

"In the village women carried bundles of wood on their head, wrapped in a rope. One woman had a brand-new rope she had bought and somebody stole it. On Sunday morning, she says to the priest, 'Please mention this in service. I'm a poor widow, please ask for the person to return it.' After the service, she asks the priest why he didn't mention the stolen rope during service. He said, 'I didn't need to. I know who has it. You can run up the hill to her house now before she gets there, and you'll find it.' She asks, 'How do you know?' The priest answered, 'She came in here. Made the cross ten times, knelt, and said Hail Marys ten times. Made ten more crosses—guilty as sin!'" Helen at this point would be laughing so hard the words of the closing punchline weren't even recognizable when they squeezed out of her lips. No matter. Her children knew the end by heart.

That night Susie peered at her father's face and grew alarmed. She'd twice witnessed fear in him. Both times he had been rushing Ma off to hospital. Now his worst fear was facing him squarely. She searched his eyes. He seemed oddly calm and rather dazed. Like he was somewhere else, like a boy caught in the wrong place at the wrong time. Her heart splintered for him, for the cold loneliness soon to descend on him.

On the 21st Helen said to her two daughters in the room, "Bring me the newest baby." As it happened, George and Gloria arrived at about that time with their three children. Laura went out to greet them and gathered the baby from Gloria's arms, saying, "Ma asked to see the youngest." In the bedroom, she sat six-month-old Denice upright on the bed within easy reach of Helen, who patted the child on the head, then proclaimed, "This one will return to the old country!"

All that day the family came, left, returned again, with and without children, and spoke in hushed tones. Somehow,

Helen bade goodbye to each grandchild. Somehow it was felt that the end was near. At first light, the phone rang again at George and Gloria's.

"She wants Gloria to pray by her bedside," Laura explained. Evidently, Helen believed that Gloria had the purest heart and craved her presence in that hour. Laura and Susie stood on either side of the bed, Joe seated next to it, when Gloria entered. Once Helen was aware of Gloria in her room, she smiled. She then turned and looked long and hard at her husband; the silent gaze between them seemed to express all that need not be said. Then she looked at the foot of her bed and said, "Ah, He is right there. Jesus has come."

CHAPTER 15

Golden Boy

Latakia - 1953

Louisa

I heard the footsteps—lots of them—before Stepan reached the hut. He was not alone. About eight boys arrived panting at our doorstep behind the little stone church and bent over to catch their many individual breaths above the hands planted on their knees. Stepan, however, did not waste a beat.

"The President has written me a letter, Mayrig!" What was he talking about?

"President of what, Stepan?"

"Syria! The President of Syria!" gulped one of the boys, body now straightened and perched at Stepan's elbow.

The boys had run from the mission school, where Stepan has been tutoring since he completed his own studies there. This was the second time such a scene occurred in the old quarter. The first had been a few months earlier, when all of Syria opened the Arabic newspaper on a Monday morning to read that the country's prized Baccalaureate had been awarded to an Armenian boy. The entire Armenian quarter of Ladehkiya had come out to the streets to gather, to exclaim, to exult in the "Golden boy," to set off firecrackers, and sell lahmajoun and kufta kabobs from arranged fire pits and makeshift tables. It had been an instant holiday for us, a nation of people that valued our education above much of what the world had to offer. Then, as now, I summoned Asadour in my head and addressed him with my private monologue:

See what your son has done! Rest assured that you survive in him, my love—in his heart and in his service. He will do great things, there is no doubt now.

There was little time to prepare for our move to Damascus. Stepan was to attend the University while at the same time he would tutor the President's children! He secured an apartment for the three of us—Manasse, Stepan, and myself. With little doubt as to the destiny of my youngest son, or of our immediate relocation, still, my teary heart limped along with our lives being torn away from Ladehkiya. True, the life I refer to and that I still mourn, has had mixed reviews. Nevertheless, the streets of the old Armenian quarter echoed a loneliness when my heels made contact with the cobblestones—a yearning for both the present and the past.

While life in Damascus was good and decent, our very existence was tentatively tied to Stepan's relationship with the President of Syria. Although, I had no doubts about my son's abilities and character, the thread of contact with such power cannot help but feel tenuous. This President took a keen interest in Stepan since winning the Baccalaureate and swept up his life so that Manasse and I saw little of him. Tutoring the palace children was his top priority, even while attending the University, both of which occurred with the President's good grace and, therefore, at his pleasure. Never one to complain, Stepan worked and studied and juggled and Manasse also worked long hours at a restaurant.

I was too idle in that city, with no purpose to fill my days. Since Damascus is a maze of ancient streets and buildings, wandering the city could have delighted me enormously except that, amidst the dominant Muslim population, it was not possible for me to do so as a woman alone. I missed teaching, missed working at all, felt almost trapped as if in a foreign country. Twice in four years, we were invited to the Presidential Palace for a rare event.

It was, of course, a symbolic honor, and the President and his wife greeted us with grace, but once we passed through the 'royal' receiving line, there was nothing else to do but stand straight in a corner of the ballroom and be glanced over. Naturally, we were dressed in the best way possible for our means and naturally, too, it could not have been sufficient. We busied ourselves studying the great hall, pillared and adorned with intricate gold leaf laced throughout the casings and moldings. The marble floor stretched before us like an ocean, and we gratefully clung to our corner and wallflower status. Mostly curious about the children, I asked Stepan where he worked with them.

"In their apartments, of course. There is a common library where they gather for joint study. But Mayrig, you would not believe the size of the children's suites! Each of them is triple the size of our apartment. The saddest thing is… they barely interact with one another."

Though the President had sent a car for us to arrive at the event, we happily declined a return ride that we might stretch our limbs, enjoy the night air, and review our impressions with one another. As is usual at important moments in my life, I thought of Asadour. Would he approve? I wasn't sure. But I was heartily glad when our lives moved on to Aleppo. Political upheaval had already veered us through three presidencies and we welcomed some stability.

Aleppo - 1960

Stepan burst in the gates and bounded the stairs, almost tripping on the broom I'd left on the landing. It was early June and the humidity in our Jdeydeh quarter of Aleppo captured the dust in droplets of moisture so that the air felt like heavy mud outside of the clean swept courtyard. I'd been sweeping the stairs for three years while my son navigated his new life.

"Mayrig! I have received the grant! The United States, Mayrig!" Now I have watched my son react with astonishing calm to each success of every goal he set for himself over these twenty-eight years. It would not appear as a shrug or an expression of irrelevancy; rather the smoothness was as a sort of inner acceptance, wisdom, that all is as it should be—win or lose. To now see him light up so emotionally at this moment was to witness a revelation. I'd not imagined what the grant application meant to him.

"Not only the Fulbright, Mayrig. I have also received the U.S. State Department Grant for Graduate Study! I can now complete the highest level of study in all the world!"

Of course, this also confirmed that our little family nucleus will cease to be a trio for a time. I knew he was going. He had submitted his resignation to the Lycee and to the University, and the Republic of Syria had already promised him full assistance to study abroad. It was known as the "Basse" and was granted with the express condition that Stepan must return and serve the government of Syria. With now three sources of funding, he could focus on degree research. Family was not included in the applicable visas, and we would wait the two or three years to be with our Stepan again. My heart burst for him and his future, even as it broke for me in my selfishness.

Only a few months earlier, my heart had wept for his disillusion. Not for the school—he loved the school, of course. My Stepan is the principal of the new Armenian high school, Karen Jeppe Armenian Lycee. (We Armenians call the school Gemaran). Students come from all around Syria, Turkey, and what is now called Lebanon, too, wishing to extend their education beyond the missionary schools of the region. They come speaking an average of four languages, since the mission schools teach English and French as well as Arabic. This is the only high school of the eastern Mediterranean that is taught in Armenian. Most of its graduates, like Stepan's cousin Kerop, move on to the American University in Beirut. Stepan was assigned the position at the age of twenty-five, fresh from finishing his degrees at Syrian University. I am told this is almost as unique an event as was his winning of the highest academic award in Syria, the Baccalaureate. Yet, in both mine and Stepan's opinion, it was his election to the United Arab Republic, as a member of the Joint National Union representing Syria at Cairo in 1960, that fulfilled a destiny never imagined.

I think of my Asadour, whose dreams of an Armenian Cilicia Republic were cruelly, flippantly dashed. How he had persevered with dignity and pride in his community, even when he chose to leave the shoe shop and Kaladouran behind for the sake of sustaining our family. How he might now marvel at the way men listen to his son when he enters a room, one of very few statesmen in Syria who can speak Arabic, English, and Armenian. His soft voice conveys a wisdom that commands attention, as heads pivot toward him and lean in to hear his words more clearly. Stepan maintains a commitment to his current community as well, serving on Aleppo's City Council and the Executive Committee of the National Union in Northern Syria. He travels often for these duties—to Damascus, Ladehkiya, and Cairo—and lectures at Aleppo University.

In May, however, he returned from Damascus with an alarming sadness. I have never seen my son so totally dejected, not before nor since, and was reminded of my husband's wavering trust in, and disappointments with, the French army and its promises to the Gamavor.

"Mayrig, it is not sustainable. For so long I've listened to my colleagues complain that Nasser is using Syria, with no intention of maintaining a partnership. I felt they were exaggerating. But I fear they were right—Nasser has gone too far..."

"In what way, Stepan?"

"He has squeezed out our officials and positioned Egyptians throughout our government. Now he is nationalizing every aspect—banks, industry, insurance… Syria is too close to dependency again—is being set up as a satellite territory for Egypt."

"And the solution, Stepan?"

"There are rumblings. I'm certain of a coup. And in that, anything may happen. If national sentiment takes hold, it may not bode well for minorities. I must resign, of course, and travel to the United States before the Basse fund disappears."

He applied quickly for international funding and was rewarded. Gratefully, my son will be spared the dramatic fall-out of our short government experiment, and may look ahead to expand his studies. I've no doubt he will return renewed to contribute to Syria in a positive way once more.

Aleppo buzzes with excitement and diverse cultures. We feel more at home here than we had in the capital city. Here the Armenian community thrives—indeed, many miracles have risen from the ashes and hallways of Armenian camps and orphanages that sustained a number of Armenian lives through the terrors against our people. Missionaries and foreign aid workers dug in their heels and provided what help they could get away with; the city was large enough to hide and protect some children and even women. Now Aleppo is alive with new hope in a modern age of possibility. Yes, Aleppo is dusty and noisy like all cities. But I am neither lonely here as I stroll the Armenian quarter, nor do I feel unsafe in other, more modern sections.

Tonight, the grandson of Asadour's cousin Khatchig joins us for a goodbye dinner for Stepan. Kerop is still a teen but has grown close to Stepan. He came from Kessab to attend the high school and is a regular in our modest apartment, which makes me happy. He hands me a small bowl of green olives from the souk nearest our quarter.

"Barev, Kerop-jan. How are your studies progressing?" I ask.

"Hello, Aunty! Guess what? My acceptance is complete! I will continue at the American University of Beirut next year. I am so grateful to Stepan, I can't imagine how to express it."

We will miss him, the only extended family we have known in Aleppo. Manasse and I will now find ourselves on our own in this ancient, yet growing city, but we will be content. I have again found work with missionaries—my perpetual angels—at the mission school of Aleppo. Unlike Ladehkiya, Damascus is fading from our present lives.

In June we decided on a trip to Kessab before Stepan's departure. Waiting in anticipation, I walked about on my own during the days that Stepan was wrapping up his affairs. Our own area, in the northwest Christian quarter of Jdeydeh, was a short walk across the wall into the Ancient City where I passed souqs and mansions, following narrow alleys and imagining visitors from the past walking these very stones at the end of the Silk

Road to trade goods from the farthest reaches of Asia. I spent an entire afternoon in Al-Madina Souq where I purchased some silk to make a dress shirt for Stepan's journey and chatted with merchants— Armenian, Alawite, Kurdish. When I came upon the soap stalls and fingered the famous Aleppo soaps, I reminded myself that most of them are actually produced in Kessab. I would wait and purchase the laurel and olive soap for Stepan's trip in the Kessab market. Exiting the souq through a khan for traveling traders, I admired the Muslim arches of the hammam across the alley and marveled at the popular custom, a curious thing. Public bathing was not an Armenian habit and I had never been inside a hammam, though our women often gathered together for grooming. Finally, I returned to Jdeydeh and visited both Forty Martyrs Armenian Church and Saint Elijah Cathedral; I offered prayers in each for Stepan's safe journey. I knew I would continue this habit for as long as he remained on the other side of the world.

Early on a Saturday morning at the end of June, we stepped on the train to Ladehkiya. From there, we arranged for transport to Kessab through the Kessab's local taxi man. But first, we wandered the Armenian quarter and walked to the little stone church and hut. Standing before it, Stepan suddenly balked.

"Let's not enter, Mayrig. Let's not go back." I knew what he was saying, and agreed.

But we did visit the mission school and there Stepan immediately caused a flurry of excitement. I was surprised that he would be recognized, even now in his late twenties, by several of the teachers. But he is their star and serves as inspiration for many students, and so was whisked away into classrooms amid clusters of admirers. Never one to enjoy attention, he was relieved to escape, and we made our way to the station and short drive to Kessab. The mountain air rewarded us as the taxi climbed ever upward.

CHAPTER 16

AMERICANS

Syracuse, NY - 1961

JOE PETER

Joe looked contentedly around the table at his large family. Each son gazing back at him had established a business of his own, amazingly. He chuckled at the memory of these boys spending hours tinkering on old parts in the barn, creating new contraptions to play with or to drive or to listen to voices on the radio. Who knew that sort of tinkering—as necessary to life on the farm as growing things—could become a stream of income to support a family? It seemed like everybody in America now wanted a working television set and three of his boys were just the ones to keep 'em working! Even George, who worked long days at Cornell University, had set up a television shop in his basement where he filled up his weekends with the tinkering! Contemplating this, he marveled: how comfortable was his new country, this Amirka! His children would have an easier time, a better life. It had been a good decision to leave the Caribbean life and keep moving, he thought. No doubt about it!

Joe pushed back his chair, ready for the requisite game of pinochle that would come as soon as his sons were ready to announce the departure from the table to their wives. He felt expansive about leaving it to them, now that he had no one to answer to, and no need to manage anything. The boys had their own relationships to navigate in their own way. It was Christmas, 1961. They were at John and Charlotte's Nottingham house in Syracuse, not the typical locale for holiday meals, which usually took place at Sam's or George's. But George had whisked his family off to Puerto Rico when the opportunity presented for him to work on—what was it?—radio astronomy at a big—the biggest—telescope in the world.

Puerto Rico! The thought of that place was a gut punch, causing a jumble of emotions. He decided to think about it later, at home in bed. Right now, he would stay present. Sam was talking....

"Family! Pa! I have a surprise! George and Gloria have sent us a recorded tape with their voices! Gather around and we can listen to them, just like they are here with us in the room."

Sam had set up a contraption, called a reel-to-reel, with two connected wheels of a flimsy brown ribbon. He turned a lever and suddenly, there was George's voice! Wives, teens, even toddlers oohed or gasped. They heard a sweet message from their Aunt Gloria and the voices of their four cousins. Everyone especially giggled at six-year-old Paula's voice singing, "My boyfriend's name is Tony; He comes from the land of baloney, with a pickle on his nose and two front toes, that's the way my story goes!"

Then it was their turn. Sam said, "Now we will record our Christmas messages, each of us, to send back to George and Gloria, so they can hear our voices. Before you kids slip away, come over here and take turns speaking into the mic. Say something to your cousins!"

Every child of talking age said something into the microphone, from the younger kids' shy words of missing someone to typical wise cracks and laughter from Joey and Lorraine. After everyone else had taken a turn, Sam nudged Joe until he punched out static syllables in his clipped accent.

"Hello, George an Gloria! How are ta kids! Tank you very much!" He teared up then. He couldn't help it.

For just a moment he imagined himself there again, feeling the humidity of the tropics, and pushed the thought out of his head. But Sam was not finished with his speeches, nor his surprises. No wonder, the pinochle game hasn't started, thought Joe.

"Pa, we got a Christmas present for you! It's an early birthday gift, too. We all went in on it...." Sam was shoving an envelope into his father's hand and the room erupted with applause, which brought the littlest ones, who had drifted into the adjacent room to play, curiously running back. Joe pulled out a long, rectangular card from inside the envelope and looked up perplexed. Sam laughed. "I bet you'd like me to read it, wouldn't you?"

Joe cracked back, "Unless you want me to use it to start the fireplace!" Laughter filled the room, but Sam waited for it to gradually die down before he pronounced, with the seriousness of an overhead announcer, "Joseph Peter. Round trip flight to San Juan, Puerto Rico. Departure February 8, 1962."

Berkeley, California - 1963

STEPAN

Stepan marveled at his new world whenever he took the time to detour the Berkeley campus and stroll along Strawberry Creek, his head so often cocked backwards to peer up the thick trunks of the Redwood trees that his neck would grow stiff. The tease of trickling water bouncing on stones and the breeze swooping up and down among the giant trees, strumming melodic drones in his ears, soothed his mind and tickled him awake. The peace he felt here was seductive, almost frightening. He could lose himself in such moments of respite away from mathematical thought, and even imagine a life here. That was the frightening part, not to be dwelt on—it was not an option for him. Sometimes, too, he pictured forays on Mount Cassius in Kessab where he had once explored the foothills with pals on summer Saturday outings. His ancestral home was so far away from the place he was in now that he felt surprised by the back and forth fluttering of his mind between places while in such a relaxed mood. This was the magic of Berkeley, but also deceptive and teasing. It felt surreal—as if all things were possible. For his colleagues and fellow students, they probably were. For now, at least, Stepan was here and decided not to obsess about life after completion of his PhD in engineering science.

Stepan was grateful that his Masters in Mathematics at Urbana, Illinois had been completed swiftly. The single winter he spent in the Midwest was enough cold to last him a lifetime; he joked of this to many of his new friends and professors. The Bay area weather was milder even than northern Syria, and Stepan felt spoiled by the adjustment. He missed his mother tremendously, his brother, too. But he sought to push thoughts of Syria from his head more and more. It was increasingly difficult to picture his future there, should he try. If he faced his emotion head on, he might identify a feeling of entrapment. But he had no choice, no voice in his future, no option for change. He had already begun to envy his colleagues, Americans and foreigners alike, free to continue carving a path through research of their own choosing. Not only were they able to follow their passions, they were certain of a future, of a government that would not waver in commitment to all its citizens. On the flip side, it was entirely possible that his duty to the Syrian government might result in any arbitrary, and wholly involuntary, assignment. In short, he was unable to envision his elusive, unknown future. It felt crippling, untenable, and completely beyond his control.

While writing his thesis, and also lecturing in Mathematics, Stepan was steeped in a research project with his advisor that thrilled him in its specificity and cutting-edge value. They were bringing together aspects of education, systems analysis, and programming for which his advisor had applied for a grant with the U.S. Civil Service Commission. Stepan did not dare imagine his deepest desire—a seed of hope—which he shoved deep down to lay dormant alongside the thoughts of his Syrian future. He could afford neither of these thoughts—the good or the bad. But the seed was lying there, nonetheless. What if? What if the grant were won and he was allowed to remain in the country long enough to complete the research? Not only had he landed in a state of total dread of his return to Syria, the opportunity to teach, to create and improve cutting-edge programs, to be a part of the progress of education—was all so intoxicating, he grew terrified of his fantasies.

Professor Dantzig invited him to lunch the next week. Stepan noted the formality with which he brought it up, but thought, perhaps he merely wants to discuss the project. The Japanese restaurant on the main drag connecting campus with the city of Berkeley was new and freshly painted, mostly in red which gave off a vague impression that it might be Chinese. Why are Chinese restaurants always red, Stepan thought. Dantzig was already seated in a booth toward the storefront window. He had even ordered! Dumplings and tempura.

"I did not want to be distracted," he explained. "I need your complete attention."

Stepan sat up straighter, pushing his bottom into the intersection of the wooden bench and the back of the booth. Knowing the uselessness of speculation and mind games, he waited for it—whatever "it" may be.

"Mr. Karamardian, I hope you will say yes to what I am about to ask you." The professor then inhaled a bite of dumpling and barreled ahead without another breath, as if he needed to release all his words at once or risk losing them. "Will you consider staying in the United States to complete our project? You would simultaneously commute to Irvine campus as a salaried assistant professor? These are the terms of the request I have made on your behalf to stay." Dantzig took another beat to study the face across from him and slowed his words to ensure they were understood. "In order to complete the work, I need you, Stepan, and this is the case I made to the U.S. State Department. I hope we might have an answer by fall."

Stepan floated out the red doors of the restaurant, not having touched a single bite on the plate he left sitting on the booth table. His apartment was only two blocks away, but he felt like wandering—even skipped a few steps—around the neighborhoods that circle the Berkeley campus, in order to absorb what he was feeling. The incredible relief. He had not wanted to admit to himself, let alone another person, the scratch that had been growing inside him since the first month at Berkeley—that he did not want to return to Syria, to leave the U.S. But because of the "Basse," he was required to go back. Had he explained that thoroughly to Dantzig? He now wondered. Was there a time limit? When such questions began to pile up, pushing to the forefront of his mind and crowding out the euphoria he had been enjoying, Stepan employed the mental discipline he had honed for almost thirty years and shut it down.

Two months later, he received the call. Two calls, actually: the first came from a jubilant Dantzig, wanting to alert him to the second call. A small portable radio, for which he had splurged, sat in his tiny kitchen. Stepan turned the knob on and was fiddling with the dials when the phone rang beside it.

"Mr. Karamardian, you are about to receive a call from the State Department. I hope it will make you as happy as it will make me...."

"Oh my, yes, sir! I would love nothing more than to work and research—and teach too—for as long as possible... before my return to Syria." Stepan gushed without shame. The deepest wish that he'd dared not hope for... could it be coming to him so easily?

"Stepan, my boy! I don't think you understand..." and for fifteen seconds Stepan's heart sank. Of course, he had jumped to conclusions, he thought, staring across the room at a clock on the wall with black numbers. But Dantzig continued, "I made a formal request with the State Department which I believe has been granted. This is not a visa extension, but for your legal residency—which can lead to citizenship if you wish to stay indefinitely! The United States needs and wants your mind, Stepan! Stepan?"

Tears came on so hard and fast, Stepan covered his eyes. When he raised his head he could no longer see the clock on the wall across the room through the blur. The grown thirty-one-year-old Armenian man from Syria had not cried since he was a ten-year-old boy—when his father disappeared from his life. Through a fog of joy, he heard himself say the thing that had lain unsaid at the bottom of everything in his world.

"I can never again set foot in Syria."

"Well then, my boy, it is best you get your mother and brother to California before this gets out. Just in case."

Within five minutes of hanging up, the phone rang again. The immigration official confirmed the information.

Stepan knew he would relive the following minutes repeatedly throughout his life. Just as the man said, "Mr. Karamardian, you have been accepted to stay in the United States," Stepan became acutely aware of words coming from the radio, sung by a man's voice soaring over the strummed chords of a guitar:

> "This land is your land, this land is my land,
> from California to the New York Island,
> from the redwood forest, to the gulf stream waters,
> this land was made for you and me!"

CHAPTER 17

JOURNEYS

Puerto Rico - 1962

JOE

He arrived in San Juan an old man. He had left it a young one, full of promise and desperation to move forward on the mainland. George collected him at the airport, and they drove west for an hour along the northern highway, the Atlantic waves visibly bobbing at numerous places where the road skirted the coastline. A whistle escaped from between Joe's teeth, and he smiled at the son he had missed for over a year.

"I'm right back where I started." He shook his head humorously at the thought and also, that he'd let it escape out loud. George was curious and glanced over, but his father wasn't inclined to elaborate just then.

The little house in the middle-class neighborhood was tucked into a circle of one-story homes off the major route through town. Gloria flung open the door with two girls close behind who he recognized as the smaller ones—Paula and Denice—and he reached into his pants pockets for the yellow wrapped packs of gum he had picked up at the airport. Gloria's hair was even whiter blonde from the Caribbean sun. Her blue eyes leapt out among the dark brown ones of her offspring, like a patch of blue sky breaking through dark rainclouds. Her laughter was infectious, like Sam's wife Ruthie, and Joe thought to himself that these sons had chosen for love and chosen well. It was good.

The next day the kids were whisked away before dawn to school across the island in a "publico" taxi driven by a dubious character named Ramon, whom George told him about. They were enrolled this year at the air force base school run by Americans to catch up on their learning, after basically losing a year at the local school taught in Spanish. Even more problematically, the public Catholicism of the island's education carved out half the school day to be immersed in religious mass ceremonies. Sending the kids to Ramey, George and Gloria now had little choice but to trust their children to questionable behaviors, detours, and the loose timing of this impulsive Ramon, who had a curious relationship with schedules. Nobody else could be found—they had tried terribly. So far, the kids always got home, thank God.

A teenaged girl arrived after breakfast. Elena literally strutted into the house. George had warned him about her, too. She had shown up one early Saturday morning, literally marched into their bedroom, and demanded a job. The couple were helpless to refuse her, though they had no clue what to do with a maid and the girl had even less clue what was expected of a maid. Elena was part of the household now, inserted into their lives with a flourish and stuck like a ton of glue. The family grew to love her, though when she fixed on a desire or a goal, there was no reasoning or turning back.

She flicked a look at the man with snow-white hair and thick, black eyebrows and said in Spanish, "About time you made it, old man!"

Joe recognized '*viejo*' and laughed outright with vigor and abandon. Her head shot up, evidently in surprise that her muttering comment had been understood, and she was hooked. She latched onto him without regard for age or the talk of the neighbors. She flirted shamelessly and grabbed his hand to hold when anyone was looking. Joe humored her and thoroughly abandoned himself to the delight of the language that tumbled recklessly from deep, forgotten senses. Joe had spoken so little Armenian over the decades that he was shocked to discover how much he missed speaking the Spanish language. It was liberating and joyful and rolled off his tongue in a way English never had. He vaguely recalled how easy it had flowed to him while still in his teens. He guessed that he fulfilled a grandfatherly role to a girl seeking a childhood.

He just kept laughing and laughing at her, calling her names and joking in a fluent torrent—words he had not thought of since he left the hills outside of Port Hune where he once pedaled his produce to islander immigrants who adored him. Or before that, the Dominicans who farmed the inland valleys on the island west of this one. His grandchildren were taken aback—shocked and truly impressed at his command of the language. After all, he barely spoke English and they had never heard him speak smoothly in a language he knew well.

Elena insisted he visit her home and take a picture with her. The faded color picture shows the two of them, standing on the hill in front of a green hut on stilts, holding hands—dark, short cropped haired Elena with smooth cocoa skin and an old man with loose pants legs and lightweight short-sleeved shirt (appropriate for the tropics) flowing in the breeze. She suggested he marry her. He only laughed at her. Surely, she was joking, as usual.

There was a nuanced tension that only someone from outside the household might neutrally observe or, in the case of Joe, instinctively feel about Elena's presence there. He knew the family had grown to care for her deeply. But of all the obstacles they—George, Gloria, and all four kids—had risen to overcome in this new culture they found themselves thrust into, the most challenging one appeared to be adjusting to Elena. Her presence required navigating a moodiness, acquiescing to a personal agenda, and for the kids, it often meant surrender in ways they were not accustomed to. Elena was a force to be reckoned with and usually got whatever she put her mind to. When that conflicted with the kids, George and Gloria used the opportunity to teach their children charity and hospitality.

Joe attempted to draw away from the kids some of the stress he sensed they took on from Elena's insatiable appetite for their attention and their possessions. He knew instinctively that his grandkids resented Elena's domination of his time and made a point to sweep them into the tricks he played on her—like the time he chased her up a ladder onto the roof. The ladder was always there—the kids used it often and lingered on the roof for the novelty of it. Elena, of course, thought he was going up after her, but he winked at the granddaughters standing by and whisked the ladder away. Stranded, Elena spewed strings of invectives loud and long enough that neighbors began to emerge onto porches to take a look. When they saw Elena pounding her fists on the roof, they laughed and laughed along with Joe and the kids. Humor is infectious, in any culture. Joe's humor transcended many of them. He felt light and grateful to have lived to this moment.

George and family took him to visit the Ramey Air Force base on the west side of the island, where the kids were attending school. Jets whizzed overhead and English words of American military families whizzed through the air. In spite of this, Joe considered how close he actually was to Hispaniola, the Dominican Republic, his introduction to the new world one island to the west. Where he had left his brother, Asadour of Bedros. Surely, his brother was no longer near these waters; if so, he could have communicated between the wars. No, there is no point speculating, Joe chided himself.

They also drove to Ponce on the southern coast, but first to the building site of the Arecibo Observatorio along the mountain road that led towards it. It was hard to imagine what the structure would look like when it was finished. The second of three towers, which loomed over a natural bowl-shaped dent in the landscape below, was being completed. How thoroughly passionate George was about his work there. He practically hummed with the radio static he listened to all day, thought Joe.

Joe's favorite times were on Saturday nights, when George set up the carport for neighborhood limbo parties. Harry Belafonte's voice crooned from a phonograph blaring through the jalousie windows of the living room. Every man, woman, and child on the entire street gathered, from infants to one-hundred-year-olds; the young dancing, the old ones fanning themselves from lawn chairs. Back home, George and Gloria had taken up square dancing. It seemed natural for them to create social environments wherever they landed—not stuffy parties meant to flaunt, but settings of welcomed joy through activity.

Joe thought of all this on the flight home. He then allowed his thoughts to float over the heads of each of his sons and daughters and acknowledge the outgoing nature of them all. And why wouldn't that be so? he mused. Their mother was the most outgoing person he knew. Helen had infused them with hospitality and inclusiveness. The family mainly had worked hard but when they partied, they did so thoroughly, welcoming all with as many as the planks and sawhorses could accommodate platters of food. The sound of steel on steel seemed to whizz from ear to ear, as he recalled tossing the horseshoes at rings, interrupted by shouts of triumph from his sons, brothers, cousins, the men from Melkia and Binghamton.

At home he settled into a routine of baking and making rounds on weekdays, delivering his signature round Syrian loaves and something he had invented that the kids called "zingos." He fried green peppers and onions with ground lamb, tucked this into rolled out cigar-shaped bread dough and finally deep fried the pieces in oil. The grandkids adored these and fought their way to the platters when he arrived anywhere. There were twenty-seven grandchildren now (that he knew of). He pretended to grow angry at anyone who claimed more grandkids than he, though this obsession with the brood was laced with humor, and he enjoyed putting on a show of competition for the kids. Helen must be proud, too, he thought, though she would have a clever comeback. Something to do with paying the price with her body. Then she would laugh and laugh. Like in the early days.

With the initiation of flying in an airplane behind him, Joe was more than willing, and sufficiently amazed, to fly again. This time it was across the country on his maiden voyage to the famous California. There had been a time, decades ago and back in Detroit, that the three brothers discussed buying an orange farm in California. But for Joe, the unease of relying on a living that involved Leo in the picture was enough for him to instinctively back away. Archie had not been so lucky, and in doing business with their younger brother, he had spent much of life troubleshooting dramas created by Leo, such as unhappy flower customers.

Joe had not once physically peeked at the California lives of his siblings, nor even that of his eldest daughter. Helen's health had superseded any thought of it. And so, in 1963, he finally walked into his Susie and Horon's Los Angeles home, where the west coast segment of the clan gathered to celebrate his presence. That, and the feel of the dry Southern California air, momentarily reminded Joe of Kessab. He quickly turned his attention to the present.

It had been decades since he had seen his brothers Archie and Leo. As busy as Susie was in her job at the hospital, thought

Joe, she managed to lay out a spread her mother would have been proud to eat. After supper, the three brothers naturally wrapped up their first evening together with a pinochle game, and included Archie's sons Nishan and Horon, who were less enamored of card playing than were Joe's sons. They were good sports, though, and sweet cigar smoke enveloped them while the conversation drifted between Turkish, Arabic, and Armenian. Archie's beloved Satinique had died just a few months before Helen's passing in 1953. Of late, he had been thinking of Syria.

"Somebody told me I should visit Kessab. Lots of folks in Los Angeles now are from Kessab and some go back. What do you think?" Archie asked. Leo just grunted. He had married late, and his Edna recently passed away. He had not thought of it. Joe Peter was more emphatic.

"John pushed me, too. I told him, 'I left ta ting back der. I'm not going back!'"

No more was to be said of Kessab, since Archie died a few months later. If Joe knew his brother was dying when he made the trip, he made no mention of it to anyone. He wept to himself at the news, silently blessed Susie for encouraging his visit, and thought to himself,

When did I start crying? Is it because I'm old?

The telegram came in 1964. It was from Hagop (Jack), Martha's eldest. Gazar had passed. Martha cried and cried for her brother Joe and would not be consoled until they wired him. She insisted on the wire, rather than a phone call. Her son Jack figured, he

later told Joe, it was because in her mind, it would be taken more seriously and demand imminent reaction that was more likely to bring him to her.

His sister Chi Chi disagreed. "Don't you see how her mind is jumbled up over the years? More likely, she doesn't even remember the invention of the telephone!"

Joe Peter took the Western Union envelope, grabbed another piece of mail from the countertop that sat waiting to be opened, and walked out the kitchen door of the small King Road house. He stepped easily over a shallow ditch into the back yard of Sam's adjoining property. A fenced off new swimming pool sprawled on the top of the slope behind the house, ignored by Joe who had swum in no waters except the Mediterranean and Caribbean Seas. He could just have easily walked the six or seven feet to the appliance store in front of his own house. But rather than interrupt Sam in conversation with a customer, he knew his daughter-in-law, Ruthie, would happily read him the message and, if needed, patiently help him navigate a response. Besides, he enjoyed the cool calm of Sam's quiet ranch house, and even reveled more at being there when the kids burst in from school and attacked him with hugs. There had lately been conversation—no, call it pleading—from Sam and Ruth about giving up the little house and joining their household. He wasn't ready.

After Ruthie read the news about Gazar and, importantly, Martha's plea, Joe helplessly confided in her.

"Damn! Poor Marta. I don't have ta money to go." The first word was muttered under his breath in the stronger Arabic version, but Ruthie had heard it enough to know its meaning.

She would have laughed in her tinny, infectious voice had Joe not looked so distressed. Distractedly, she opened the second envelope that he had already forgotten about.

"Pa! This is from the gas company. It says here they want to buy an easement from you."

"Wat is tis eezement?" but she was still reading. When she finished, she looked up, beaming from ear to ear.

"Pa, your problem is solved right here. The gas company needs a slice of your property to install a gas line up King Road. They'll pay you two hundred dollars! Maybe you can get it right away and go to Detroit."

The funeral was on Saturday. Marta sat on a blue settee in the church parlor, surrounded by her sister Mary, her two sons and daughter. Martha was half blind by now and Mary, too, had become blind. Four of her grandsons, Chi Chi's brood of boys, were assigned to watch for Joe's taxi. Two of them continually raced in and out of the door to the sidewalk, with the eldest, Harry, lying to their distraught grandmother.

"He's almost here, Grandma! I can see his taxi coming up the street!" Harry exclaimed, perhaps one too many times. But he had too often witnessed mental descents to a depth of sadness that resulted in her hospitalization and was panicked by Martha's current fragility.

Each time a church staff entered and suggested they begin the service, Martha wailed anew. It seemed as if they stalled for hours. Finally, Joe's taxi pulled up to the curbside where the door was thrust open by several very tall nephews who literally pushed Joe inside—desperate for their Nana to stop hurting. Martha collapsed in her brother's arms.

In winter, Sam and Ruth convinced him to move in. He was alarmed by the onset of sudden weakness, especially his shortness of breath, but hid such thoughts from his son's family. Sam and Ruth's kids called him Poppy, instead of Jido. They were a rambunctious bunch, even though three of the four were girls. Watching their energy and good natures was the best medicine for his ailments, but he tired so easily. He finally agreed to be driven by Ruth to a doctor, followed by multiple tests.

By summer, the results were in. When the doctor asked him for how long he had smoked, he replied honestly.

"Seven years."

"Oh, you've only smoked for seven years?" The doctor seemed puzzled. "Your lungs should not look like this—"

"No, since I'm seven years old!" Now the man exhaled and leaned back in his chair.

"Well, that explains the lungs—black as hell and all given out!" This cancer doctor was not sympathetic, but Joe didn't mind that.

As family rallied around him, Joe studied his sons and daughters. He saw them daily. Oddly, he saw less of his grandchildren lately, as if the parents wished to shield them from impending death. But it turned out to be a matter of visitation rules at the new lakeside hospital. Children had to be snuck in and so it happened less and less. That was his only regret about the final months which dragged out to the end of 1965. Jake's Hazel was head nurse in Emergency and she checked in on him constantly. Idle time was such a rarity for eighty-year-old Joe, even since Helen's passing. He had filled his days with baking and family—and always pinochle with his sons. Each one of them was happy in their life, fulfilled and dedicated to wives and children. Some of them loved golf. George loved the University for which he worked and remained very involved. Susie was also a head nurse now, but she took time to fly east to visit with him. Laura thrived in her farm life. The other boys owned businesses. Joe sighed.

He worried for Martha and Mary, now widows, but at least they had each other. It was a cliché to think it, he knew, but still he wondered if he would be connected once more with Nishan and Archie, and his long lost Jirgis and Zaha. He wondered if brother Asadour was alive and living somewhere in Brazil or Argentina. Surely, he would have made his way somewhere? Or was he gone, too, by now? He had no doubt that Helen was waiting for him, ready to scold or exclaim on some silly issue, chin thrust up and forward. He saw the clear form of his mother, cooking at the stone wall in Kaladouran, as she did before the big move to Ladehkiya. Her head turned toward him and smiled, and he knew.

Two more scenes invaded his consciousness before he drifted away. In one, at Kaladouran, a lamb roast permeated the hillside with its spices. Words in Kessabtsi dialect filled the air with its cadence. Family glowed and laughed all around him—family members who had existed only one decade longer than his overnight disappearance from the old country, one decade longer on earth before being marched off toward deserts to die… all the faces and laughter that he had pushed from his conscious mind over the years, in order that he might function for the living… all of them were there under the grapevine trellis. Uncles, aunts, baby cousins, all of them. He heard them call, "Hovsep-jan!"

The last scene arrived in his mind with gentleness and lingered… at the big farm at the crest of Peter Road in South Danby, all the children at home, none of them still babies. They were gathered around the stove, Helen holding court, telling one of her stories but barely getting through it—Helen laughing so hard at what she was supposed to say, she couldn't spit out the words that were choking inside her mouth. Thick auburn hair framed the glowing face. Beaming face. Joy gushed from laughter gathering around her….It was a good scene to take with him to sleep.

CHAPTER 18

This Land

San Francisco - 1965

Stepan

Stepan took plenty of time to look around the room. He was used to large gatherings of diplomats, and more recently, of students. This was different in more than one way. He was less fluid at social events. But the hall full of Armenians at St. Gregor's Armenian Church, San Francisco, was comforting in many ways—it was home! The echoes bouncing off the walls and ceiling contained a mash-up of varying Armenian dialects that included Kessaberen, minor melodies of an oud and violin, and the drone of a duduk. Round tables seating eight to ten guests made way for a parquet dance floor in front of the musicians. Some guests, particularly elder Armenians, were already on the floor moving in unison, grasping hands, and following the direction of alternating men waving white handkerchiefs. Stepan cast his eyes about for Papken, a student from Latakia he had recently run into, but his eyes rested on a woman—or girl, actually.

She was seated alone, back straight, dark hair teased and turned up at her shoulders... an exquisite creature who appeared confident and not at all awkward about her solo status at the table. Rather, she looked about with curiosity and interest, as if she were seated in a dark cinema, absorbed in a picture show. Stepan tore his eyes from her reluctantly and miraculously locked them with Papken, who stood across the room and now nodded symbolically at him. In an instant Stepan understood the boy's meaning. This is the sister Papken had mentioned, when he informed his former tutor about the New Year's Eve dinner dance at the church. Stepan looked back at the girl just as his mother, Louisa, caught sight of her as well.

Seta

Seta did, in fact, feel confident in the new dress. Her hair felt just right, too, teased at the top of her head and flipped up just below her chin, the way Annette Funicello wore it in a picture show she had just seen. Her brother Papken had brought her and her sister to the New Year's Eve banquet, their first public event since arriving in San Francisco one month earlier. At eighteen, she was breathlessly taking in the new world in which she found herself. She was also losing no time fantasizing about new possibilities—especially medical school. But for the moment, her thoughts laced with excitement and body relaxed, she was unaware that she had been stabbing her fork at a tiny morsel on the plate before her, when a soft voice said in her ear, "You know, even the Queen of England is allowed to eat chicken with her fingers."

She swung her head around and desperately tried to place the face leaning in to her own. She was unused to being caught off guard and had never in her life known how to flirt—nor what the concept meant. She realized now she was stammering with confusion and the older boy, or rather man, was laughing—but not unkindly. It took some continuing banter for her to place him, but once she did, her memories flooded—this boy at her home to tutor her brother Papken... Papken who was now rapidly approaching the table to embrace him. She recalled the talk of him, a success story, pride of the entire Armenian communities of two countries—even from her own father—for the boy who had captured the imagination of the Syrian President. Her thoughts would have continued had not another voice interrupted, from someone who appeared at her other side.

"Seta, you have become a beautiful lady!" An old woman barely reaching Seta's shoulders, now that she had respectively risen to stand, was unfamiliar and yet... somehow, safe and welcoming. "I washed your diapers when you were a baby!" laughed the elderly Louisa.

Seta's eyes bulged in their sockets. But Stepan was holding out his hand and, looking mutely from mother to son, she took it and allowed herself to be swept onto the dance floor.

Seta dreamed of medical school. She had been raised to bring honor to her family and medical school was the path she chose to do this. She had never dated—knew nothing of dating. She was not ready when Stepan visited her father in February to ask permission to take her to dinner. Her parents, however, were ecstatic. They not only adored him, but already considered him family, further confusing her. When she experienced the first kiss, she rushed to tell him her plans for school, panicked that they might get swept away in romance.

"That's a great idea!" said Stepan. "Why don't we get married; I work and you can go to school."

Again, she wasn't ready. She thought about it for months, unsure, unwilling to detour. Meanwhile, Stepan remained constant in her line of vision: so loving, caring, brilliant, family-oriented, respected by the community, responsible. He was sophisticated, cultured, educated—everything she strived for herself. People listened to his deep opinions about… just about anything. Heads turned when he walked into a room. He took care of his mother and brother… Over time, she became attached in a way that she could not resist, however long she continued to try—and it was okay. On July 11, 1965, Seta agreed to marry the golden boy. Louisa lived with them from the beginning.

New York State - 1968

Stepan and Seta

Stepan and Seta boarded a plane in June of 1968 for New York. Neither had been to that side of the country, other than passing through airports upon their initial arrivals to the United States. Since their first child arrived when Seta was nineteen, there had been little time for an extended honeymoon. Seta was again pregnant, about five months so, and the window of opportunity was closing in again. It was a last chance for some years to come and they carved out several weeks to explore. After four days in the city, they rented a car.

Stepan wanted badly to find his relatives in New York. He knew that their surname was Peter, that Karamardian had been dropped and now lost to this branch of the family. Though his mother Louisa had once met Archie in Los Angeles, she had not been in touch—since Asadour's correspondence with Joe in Michigan—and she knew that Joe had long returned to upstate New York. The couple headed north to the thruway and took in the surrounding scene that surprised so many who drove through the state. Endless shades of green farmland was seldom a picture that came to the minds of those who had never been to New York and tend to imagine skyscrapers from one end of the state to another. The landscape took Seta's breath away. She could watch it for days.

Stepan, on the other hand, was on the lookout for phone booths at every exit past Albany, and pulled up to each one he spotted, making the trek across the state slow going. Some of the phonebooks were thin, with mostly yellow pages—very few white pages with illegible, small, printed columns of names in black print. The name 'Peters' was so common it overwhelmed. He focused on looking for the singular 'Peter,' followed by Joseph.

Suddenly a bang came from outside the car that caused her heart to race. Both Stepan and Seta jumped to the conclusion that a helicopter hovered just above them. When he tried to pull over, Stepan was surprised at how difficult it was to maneuver the car to the shoulder of the road. Swinging his long legs out of the cramped driver's seat, he stood and looked upward.

"Nothing there, Seta!"

Seta climbed out and walked to the back of the car—and instantly spotted it. The back passenger tire had deflated to the ground, to the very edge of its rim. Stepan approached and looked down. He folded his arms, looked up and down, and stood silently. He then paced a little ways behind the car while other cars whizzed past. Seta looked at him and, though she tried very hard to hold back, could not help but burst out laughing, "Stepan! You don't know how to change a tire, do you?"

She found it hysterical that this brilliant, acclaimed husband of hers had no practical skill whatsoever; she simply could not stop laughing. Stepan's cheeks burned; whether from anger or shame she couldn't tell. Gradually, she pulled herself together and shifted to a helpful tone.

It was about fifteen minutes before a car slowed and pulled up behind them, a truck, blue and high off the ground. A brawny man climbed out and asked if he could help. Stepan stood by and helplessly watched while the young man exchanged the tire with the spare one from inside the trunk. He wished the man would ask him to hand him something—a tool or hubcap—anything to participate. But the man was self-sufficient and also refused an offer of money.

"Nah, just doing the neighborly thing," he drawled in the flat accent that placed him squarely from upstate New York, though the couple could not know this. He was gone in seconds.

The signs along the highway gave mileage countdowns to various cities and towns. Back on the highway, Stepan grew excited when he read aloud the next series of towns—Rome, Utica, Syracuse…

"Utica! Utica! Seta, that sounds like the place mother thinks Uncle Hovsep lives!"

In Utica, they found a station phone booth with a very thick book inside, so heavy he had to swivel its dangling mass from the chain attached, upwards onto the booth's metal ledge to get it open. The list of P's took over twenty pages. Once more, there were six pages of Peters, but no Peter and no Joseph, or Hovsep, or even Yussef. No trace.

They had a cup of coffee at a diner next to the booth and ordered some pie. Stepan was quiet, deflated. Seta knew how disappointed he was, that he had chosen this destination as a sort of mission to honor his father. Refreshed and resigned, the couple returned to the car and continued on the New York Thruway to Niagara Falls and a belated honeymoon.

Neither of them could know the mistake—the same mistake made by young Hovsep, the first known Karamardian in the United States from Kessab, who arrived, in error, at Ithaca, rather than to certain job opportunities that had summoned clusters of Middle Eastern immigrants to that other town… called Utica. They could not know that the mistake was one of pronunciation—of an *odar*.

EPILOGUE

Myth and Mystery

Ithaca - 2023

Author

My mother was *odar*. I know this because of something I found years after her death, among piles of paperwork. It read like a term paper—an essay—that she had written for her Tuesday Club (a local literary club). I discovered the word, its meaning, and its meaning to her through her own description. The title of her essay was "Odar." It paid homage to Armenian—and all— immigrants, really. She did not write about herself, but her words caused personal scenes to flash in my head.

When Gloria Peter headed across the country on a train, circa 1945, with her exotic new bridegroom, nobody in the Nebraska community she left behind had ever heard the words 'Armenian' or 'Syrian.' She found herself deposited into a New York farmhouse full of people resembling, and as passionate as, her George. They erupted in noise and action at any given moment, arms gesturing for articulation with every verbal outburst. It was she who was strange and different: a mild-mannered, blue-eyed angel of gentleness from another world, under a halo of sun-colored hair! Her mother-in-law burst into tears at the sight of this odd vision. What good would this tiny creature be on a farm? But the story told is that Helen, my Sito, came to appreciate the petite Gloria when canning season came around and she discovered her daughter-in-law's hands were small enough to slip fully inside the pickling jars for cleaning.

"Otherness" eventually fades to curiosity when cultures are thrown together in the kinds of communities where upward mobility is tangible and hard work rewarded. Such was the case with the first generation of Syrians, bit by bit, beginning (in our family) with Joe and Helen, followed by the first war and rescue and immigration of Joe's sisters. The Finns of Peter Road, and the Italians of South Hill with whom Jido worked were, in their new local environments, as much '*odar*' as he. They created their own communities and perpetuated their own customs while gradually integrating among the wider world of Ithaca and its little corner of their new world. Many foreign communities of immigrants were established by the end of the first war. By the second war and the second generation it called up, nobody was crying over integrated marriages which just one generation earlier, would have been unfathomable in either the old or new world. All but one of my uncles served their new country in that war, along with fellows of every religion and culture who thus far called the United States home. Pre-war, their eldest brother, John, had been expected to marry among "his own." The rest returned from service with American wives—and without argument. The family story had evolved.

This "story" I have spent a lifetime seeking has come to symbolize for me a triad of life's sections. At the beginning, I was a teenager with the fearlessness of youth. I could afford the idealism that the quest for the story provided, before I learned to be overwhelmed by its impossibility. The middle process symbolized the knowledge that I needed more: more info, more time, more details, more of everything, anything, before I could begin to write. Such knowledge was full of anxiety and yearning, and often paralyzed me.

The final process came only after giving myself permission to begin writing without answers, without mysteries solved, by embracing some naïve brand of faith that the answers will come through the action of putting pen to paper. (And yes, some of them did.) This process of action then tweaked to an even sharper version…or vision: that I'll get what I need from the writing, regardless of answers.

And did I? Well, there are some mysteries still unsolved. It took a long time but eventually, I grew comfortable with that. I do feel I got what I needed. And still do. Curiously, even in the last revision stages, more plotline twists and discoveries appear and continue to be solved. Perhaps the act of releasing this story to the public will attract even more missing links. But it was basically an act of surrender that let it unfold.

Just as Dad's leaving the earth closed one world for me and opened up another, discovering the loss of Louisa's journal (from Seta) offered a similar gift. After decades of waiting for its revelations, it was, simply, not to be. So I closed that chapter of waiting and allowed myself to invite creativity to the table, filling in gaps of known details with imagination, to complete the tale. I was now free to begin.

Although the major mysteries that have consumed me were not solved, I learned, from my search for them, something of resilience. Beginning with silence—the choice Mary made to live. She would not, could not, tell her story. Her lips were sealed from the time she stepped off the boat onto U.S. soil. While Martha told bits of her story, which are incorporated into this book, Mary's choice was elusive. Some minor mysteries were solved by digging, others evoked certain reasonable guesses, such as the Simon's connections to Syria's missionaries—very likely at the core of Mary's rescue. Such a connection satisfies my lifelong curiosity; that the Karamardian brothers would have arranged a marriage for their sister to a Syrian, rather than to an Armenian. Any threads between the Simon family and Joe and Leo Peter allowed the story of the marriage to unfold naturally in my imagination. As for Mary's actual ordeal, it need not be imagined. I decided to honor the silence she chose to take to her grave and highlight the triumph. And I have no doubt that this is *her* choice, not mine.

My grandmother's sister, and the existence of a niece hinted at in a later communication that is not included in this telling—these are lost forever—clueless. Vivid imagination can draw me to the island of Dominica and a fantasy of offspring existing there still. But with no names to guess at and guide research, likely no records at all, there is no point at which to begin, nor even a certainty of existence, past or present. I fear a single chance for connection may have been lost with my grandfather's skepticism. Then again, it could have been a scam—like so many at that time. There was no certain knowledge that Helen's sister had even left Syria and yet, could be as possible as it is unlikely. Aunt Laura died insisting it was true. She spoke of a second letter and a picture sent of a girl, her cousin. Nobody else talked about it, other than a brief mention by John. But then, they had been the only ones at home during the time when the letters came.

The mystery of my great uncle Asadour (Joe's brother) is still as elusive as it was for the duration of my grandfather's lifetime. However, with hints from a psychic (I left no stone unturned), I came to the likely conclusion that Asadour never made it to South America. Here is where my imagination went with the clues offered: Asadour of Bedros, Jido's brother, was gravely ill for several years after his brother's departure for the mainland. He intentionally hid the fact from Hovsep to ensure he would not ruin his brother's mission to reach New York. The gift offered up to me from this source was that he had died in the tropics, in the tender care of a gentle woman who loved him platonically. The truth remains unknown, but this theory is as reasonable as any other. And oddly, the method infused me with a vision of Asadour's character and personality. I "felt" him tell his part in the story, up to a point… and I received an impression that he wanted me to know he could have been one of the great Arabic poets.

Mysteries or no, some myths to which I was privy and that had perpetuated throughout two generations, turned out to mislead. In order to understand this family from which I sprang, I tried to dig away, prod for potential answers lurking from the very beginning. I learned that our family suffered a universal symptom: that human emotions cause both misinformation and presumption that can last for generations. These can also transform culture or create distrust, too often via the "pick and choose" method. For example, my Jido picked and chose who to associate with the moment he landed in the Dominican Republic. He also expanded his heart over the course of his children's lives as they taught him to soften the edges that entrapped him. The ability to transform transcended to next generations—I witnessed my own father soften and expand as necessary to allow love to grow, just as his parents had done. Susie and John, Laura and Dad all shared their growth with me through versions of their witness.

But some of their attitudes continued to puzzle me—even after they had passed on— certain points they made every time a subject came up. Laura and John continued to bring up Sito's dislike of Ameen Simon, and push the myth of Muslim to Christian conversion—as it turns out, without a shred of evidence. Forced to confront this attitude in order to solve the mystery of Mary's marriage in light of everything I learned from Armenian communities (and unlikely intermarrying), I now realize that I never took that statement at face value. Either I didn't quite believe it, or something didn't add up. The longer I pursued the mystery that was Mary's life, the more suspicious I became. In this case, my instincts proved correct.

I considered the history of grudges in my large and colorful family. At different times of spats or division between one or another uncle, one or another cousin, my father often acted as peacemaker. But some resentments could last for years. I have witnessed a number of long-standing grudges among extended family members that were so ridiculous in basis, that it became second nature to laugh them off. After all, aren't all grudges based on myth and misunderstanding? Perhaps. But not so funny in larger contexts: the Middle East, Armenia and Azerbaijan, Ukraine, all of today's tinder boxes. The wars of the world have usually been ignited this way.

It was in thinking about this, as relates to my family, that I was able to fill in some blanks. Small discoveries continued to debunk long-held perceptions and launch new suspicions of misinformation. I wanted to squeeze out every clue, discover each detail, and document a factual version that evaded fiction. Even when I caught myself creating imagined scenes, I rebelled, horrified. What was that resistance about? To the imagining, which, of course, was ultimately inevitable. Fiction. At first, it felt dishonest, presumptuous, misleading. I wondered if it dishonored the memory of my ancestors to assign certain attitudes or assumptions of motivation. It took repeated failures, surrenders, and anticipated opening of doors and windows into the past being firmly shut in my face (Louisa's lost journal), to finally succumb to the forces that be and accept that I must begin filling in cracks from visions in my head and flex creative license.

It was hard. I continued to resist the currents where my imagination wanted to soar. Was I going too far? If I assign such and such a thought to that character—an actual ancestor who walked this earth and made their own choices—choices which ultimately caused my existence and therefore held value priceless beyond reason—if I did so, would I be creating another form of "misinformation?" That is a word that my body has learned to recoil from in revulsion. Even after the psychic summoned instruction from the two ancestors shrouded in mystery (Mary Karamardian Simon and Asadour Bedros Karamardian) who sent me permission from the ether of space and time, in my glass sunroom, mandating with humor (Asadour) or candor (Mary) that I "fill in the blanks" to tell their story from their hints—even this left me hesitant, timid, unworthy, horrified at the prospect of implying, imprinting my own fantasies upon those well-lived (or, in Asadour's case, short-lived) souls.

Fear intensified because the more I interviewed, the more I researched, the more I discovered discrepancies between facts and the information passed on by my "sources" (aunts and uncles with their own presumptions and biases). This developed into more fear—of assigning incorrect meaning to actions of the forbearers, of perpetuating or inventing misinformation onto pages, forever establishing new "truths" that, in fact, are impossible of knowing. But that's just it: THERE IS NO WAY OF KNOWING. Therefore, there is no way of telling their story without "imagining the rest." So, I took a breath, a lot of breaths, and went there.

Most of the story arrived outlined in anecdotes, details, and some (very few) documents. The family 'eyes' captured my imagination from the beginning: the photo of 1911 leaves an impression of wandering eyes in Nishan and Martha. Leo and Mary lived into the late 1970s, Mary blind at the end. Martha lingered another decade, partially blind, and diagnosed with a condition called Petimtis pigmentosic. I will always wonder if that was a genetic condition. It was said that Asadour was denied entry for his eyesight. Quite possibly it was the true condition that was presumed to be trachoma and barred Asadour from entering the United States in 1904. This is an easy blank to fill in, requiring little more than my reasoning. Each of the Karamardian siblings who made it to "Amirka" documented long and happy lives. The fate of eldest brother, Nishan, witnessed only by the littlest sister, Martha, was undoubtedly embedded into the mental trauma that she endured for a lifetime. And every aunt, uncle, and extended relative who made it to Amirka, spoke of the "lost brother in South America." These are facts. These are traumas. And these are triumphs. The traumas co-existed with long lives and long memories.

There are moments when I consider it would be easier to work in pure fiction, create new characters on a blank page, and invent human emotion with all its misunderstandings and triumphs. But whenever I do, my soul reaches for the characters I know; they are more alive, more human and messy and complicated than any I could make up. The twisted fate that snakes along for generations unwinds out of simple misunderstanding into nuanced bigotry at worst, and misguided assumptions at best. And then there are glorious moments of human connection that survived decades of storytelling in all its varied versions. My father's telling of Jido knocking on the door of Ithaca's Presbyterian Church to arrange for Jake and Hazel's marriage, of the door being answered by none other than his childhood friend Walter, from the mission school in Syria. I loved that story even more than his accidental arrival by train at "Itaka" instead of Utica, because a conductor had misunderstood his accent. These miracles of accidental choice and events are beyond comprehension. Therefore, I worship any detail, any tiny clue or knowledge about any ancestor. Every single one has impacted in multiple ways.

I always thought that my Sito's proclamation—that I would return to the old country— would come true. In fact, I never doubted it until the Syrian wars and troubles of the 21st century. In the mid-70s my dad and I wrote to the embassy for visas, preparing for the long-awaited visit to Kessab. But at the time, war in Lebanon prevented the journey connection through Beirut. The only available connection was to travel to Istanbul and enter Syria from Turkey. Dad would have none of it, and I did not question his judgement. We would wait until Turkey could be avoided; we felt a natural impulse that I can't put my finger on. I don't think it was fear as much as an indulgence in inherited prejudice that I accepted quite naturally as a young adult having grown up with the horror stories witnessed by my relatives. This was even before I knew of the existence of the living Karamardians, not to mention the victims. The extended family that Jido had left behind in Syria were mere ideas in my head. Back then, I knew only of my great aunts' ordeals and even those were mere whispers, void of detail. Yet, I was willing to "inherit" bias and judgement based on whispers and family attitudes.

Today I am wiser, or jaded, enough to know that the kinds of events that precipitated these emotions still exist in earnest. Genocide not only did not fade into the annals of history, but it has become as commonplace as the perpetuity of its denial. So too, my heart breaks daily in witness to systematic injustice and worse, denial, in the war against race right in my own country. So, too, it breaks for the race against war, or the multiple wars already raging in our 21rst century. With new victims every day.

In 2001, my father co-hosted a seminar at Cornell University called 'Theology of Crime' together with author Dr. E. Scott Ryan. Dad spoke specifically about the Genocide. At the end of the session, as the audience began to disperse, I watched a student, from the row in front of me, stand up and stammer,

"It isn't true! That did not happen. It could not have happened! I would know it." He was visibly upset. There were several students from Turkey, and they were deeply offended at the information my father had shared about Armenian treatment at the hands of the Ottoman Empire. I watched as an elderly man rose from another row and angrily cry,

"Don't tell ME it didn't happen. My father died on the march!" He then stoically marched out with the aid of his cane, while those of us remaining stood stunned for a moment. Then our eyes turned once more to the Turkish student. My dad came to him, gently took his arm and said quietly,

"I am sorry, son, but my family is witness to the events I describe, my grandfather and uncle killed, my aunts taken as slaves. You were not taught about it in school, I know that. The facts are not taught in your country, but the marches, the murders… they are real, witnessed and documented."

I think of that boy, that young student, hearing of this for the first time. I flash back to first hearing about Jim Crow in the 7th grade social studies unit on the Civil Rights movement, on the very same day I looked up the word "Armenian" at

Tompkins County Library and read of the horrors that befell Jido's people—*my* people, I came to realize. I found them, my people, at least some of their names. Countless others marched to Dei Zor, Aleppo, Sinai, Hamas or Amman, Jordan. Over a million deaths. Children taken, raised as Turks, never to know their heritage. Archeological sites of ancient Armenia, Artsakh, and near our original homeland of Van and atop Mount Aqra (both now part of Turkey) from the slopes of Kessab, hundreds of Armenian churches destroyed, the fading memory of a race, a culture that had thrived in Anatolia before Romans, Mongols, Marmelukes, or Seljuk Turks, let alone Ottomons.

Denying a culture, an inheritance, is nothing new—or even old. In the "new country" in which Jido (Joe Peter) carved out a life for his family—my country—it rears an ugly head again and again. On the news I hear of Holocaust deniers and mass murderers, and even state government attempts to whitewash historical fact, to eliminate real history, to pamper and soothe and cater to the comfort of an established white race that finds it inconvenient to acknowledge the sordid events of our world—events that include slavery and genocide and terror. Things that happen cannot be erased. Attempts to erase truth intentionally stifle growth and evolution. In Turkey it is illegal to utter the word 'genocide' in public. Imagine that!

Why doesn't the world panic when history is whitewashed? My despair seeks a solution and the only one I can think of is this: all we can do—and this is crucial—is to keep the stories alive. So I submit this story, the one I know. We never did make it to the old country, Dad and I. I never made it, missed any chance to, leaving my grandmother's prophecy empty and unfulfilled. I doubt now that I will ever see a laurel tree in Kessab, or Melkia, or set foot anywhere in Syria. Perhaps Sito's premonition was meant figuratively. My "return" would be in the form offered on these pages.

That is the best I can do.

I often wonder what my ancestors' reactions were, or might have been, to injustice? No activism, no words, no telling. Perseverance, yes. Triumph, yes. How? I guess it's personal. Survival can be personal. Jido's story did NOT go like this: Leave old country. Arrive in America. Achieve great success. In those versions, family is usually a side note, if mentioned at all. Although, he "sort of" did those things, I don't know what his meaning of success was, or if it is relevant. I imagine that if I could ask my Jido today how he thinks he evolved, how he sees his life, he might answer, "Why do you make it so complicated?"

Sometimes, the story is just to stay alive. Sometimes it is to save others. Sometimes it becomes the next thing: to serve family and community, to improve the lives of others.

Joe Peter did that. He managed to support family, extended family, and community through difficult times—wars, depression, etc. It's true. I suppose he believed that as long as he could maintain a garden, he could supply what was needed—a theme that endured through his life all the way to the end, when food was no longer a challenge, and baked bread was all that was left for him to offer.

It was that simple. And that beautiful.

Peters Family Has Five Sons and Daughter in Army

Ithaca, March 10—Five sons and a daughter of Mr. and Mrs. Joe Peter eof Willseyville are serving in the U. S. armed services.

Three of the boys are in the Air Corps.

Sgt. Jacob Peter, stationed at McKeesport, Pa., entered the service in March, 1942, and is now an airlone mechanic and crew chief.

Sgt. George Peter is now stationed at William Field, Chandler, Ariz. He has been in the service since August, 1942.

Sgt. Samuel Peter donned a uniform in February, 1943, and is now a radio technician in the Air Corps stationed at Bakersville, California.

Now stationed on Staten Island, Sgt. Mitchell Peter entered the service in March, 1944.

Pfc. Moses Peter, who enlisted in April, 1944, is now overseas and his parents have just had word of his arrival in Belgium.

Lt. Hazel Robertson Peter, an Army nurse, is stationed at the Army Hospital at [illegible]

Peter Brothers News clip 1945

Left to right: Pfc. Moses Peter, Sgt. George Peter, Sgt. Jacob Peter, Sgt. Samuel Peter, Sgt. Mitchell Peter, missing from photo Lt. Hazel Robertson Peter

George and Helen Peter, South Danby farm

Laura Peter birthday Dinner

Left to Right: Mitch, Mitch mother-in-law, Helen, Pat with Mitchie (on lap), Gloria (pregnant), Laura standing, Susie with Stephen (on lap), Lois, Moses, George, Mikey, Joe

Joe and sisters Detroit circa 1960

Left to Right: Garboushian (first name unknown), Gazar Karagozian, Martha Karamardian Karagozian, Joe Peter (Karamardian), Mary Karamardian Simon

The Peter daughters and wives
Left to Right: Hazel, Lois, Susie, Laura, Charlotte, Gloria, Pat, Ruthie

Stepan Karamardian (professional photo)

GLOSSARY

NAMES, PLACES AND THINGS IN ODAR WITH VARIOUS SPELLINGS

Amirka; (pronunciation for America by first generation Armenians)

Kessab, Kasap, Kesap, Casab, Casbis; town northwesternmost in Syria, on Turkish border, until years was exclusively, and is still predominantly, Armenian; named Casabelle and Casabella by first Crusaders

Latakia, Lattakia, Ladehkiya
(Kessabtsi pronunciation), Al Ladhiqiyah Port City in Northwest Syria; ancient name Laodice

Kaladouran, Karadouran; coastal village of Kessab, northwest Syria on border with Turkey

Beirut, Beyruth, Beyrout; major city in Lebanon

Tartus, Tartous

Junieh, Jounieh

Port Hune (pronunciation of Port Huron by first generation Syrians, Armenians) in Michigan, U.S.

Itaka, Ithaca (pronunciation by Joe Peter) in Finger Lakes region of New York on Cayuga Lake

J'abal A'qra, Jebbel Akra, Mount Cassius; mountain of Kessab

Jabal Mussa, Musa Dagh, Kizil Dagh; name for mountain and village of and near Kessab

Iskenderun, Alexandretta; (modern name) city in Turkey near border of Syria

Aintab; Gaziantep (Turkish name)

Constantinople; Istanbul (modern name)

Melkia, B'Melki, kfar melki; costal village near Lebanon (residents called themselves Syrian circa 1900)

Barlum Monastery, Ballum, Barlahoy, Barlaam; (believed to be founded by St. Barlaam)

Legion d'Orient, Armenian Leggionaires, Gamavor; names for the group of Armenian fighters WW1

Gamavor; volunteers, freedom fighters in Kessab after the war who patrolled and protected Kessab area

Shushan, Shoushan (Lily, name in Armenian and Hebrew)

Elisa, Alice

Armine, Armenouhi, (Armen, male version)

Asadour, Asadur

Ameen (family spelling), Amin (usual Arabic spelling)

Bedros, Boutris, Bete, Peter; Armenian, Greek, Arabic, English versions

Hovsep, Youssef, Youssif, Jose, Joseph, Joe; Armenian, Arabic, Spanish, English versions

Khatchig, Hatchig, Archie

Boghos, Paul

Laura, Zaha, Zahia, Zahea, Florence (meaning flower, Arabic versions)

Henna, Hana, John

Manas, Manasse, Leo

Moses, Mose, Mussa, Moussa, Moosey (nickname in Peter family)

Marta, Martha

Mary, Mariam, Maryam

Louise, Louisa, Louiza, Lousine

Nishan, Nishon, Mitchell

George, Giragos (Armenian), Jirgis (Syrian)

Yunnus, Younus, Yunus (Arabic) Yunis (Greek)

Tzaghir, Dzaghir, Tsaghig, Kitcha, Haigha, Zarig, Zaghig; (meaning flower, Armenian version female)

Kamor, Ataturk; 1923 took control as leader of Turkey

Kibbe, kibbee, kibbeh, kufta (Armenian version); baked mix of lamb with pine nuts and bulgar

Lubi, loobi; green bean and tomato stew, usually with chunks of lamb

Lamajoun, lamajoon, Lahmajoun; meat pies on flat bread made with ground meat, onions and peppers

Koussa, kousa, cusa (squash, zucchini, usually stuffed with meat and rice)

Babagnoush, babaganoush (eggplant)

Shadiyeh; Arabic word for pilaf

Shankleesh, tchingleesh; a cheese spiced and coated with zatar, a middle Eastern spice

Sourkig , Armenian pizza

Dolma, dolmades (Greek) tolma, sarma (Armenian); rolled grapeleaves, stuffed with meat and rice

Pigegh; Armenian olive oil bread twisted in knot shapes

Baklava, paklava; type of pastry layers with nuts and syrup, cut into diamond shapes

Boorma; version of baklava with nuts and syrup inside rolled pastry layers and cut in cigar shapes

Smeed; pastry cake made with farina

Hayrig; Armenian for father

Mayrig; Armenian for mother

Jihdo, Jido, Jid, Jidi; Arabic for grandfather, my grandfather (our version Jido)

Jida, Jidehti, Sito; Arabic for grandmother (our version, Sito)

Shukran, shookran; Arabic for thank you

Yallah, yella; Arabic for come on, let's go

Kee-fek, kee-fik; Arabic hello

Huffla, mahrajan; Syrian festival

Effendi; man of education in Ottoman Empire

Gendarme; officer of authority, such as police

Tonir; oven

Odar; Armenian for "other, stranger, foreigner"

Jan; a term of endearment in Armenian, i.e. Louisa-jan or Stepan Jan (i.e. Louisa, dear)

Inch bes es?; Armenian for How are you?

Shad lav em, park asdouzo; Armenian for I am fine, thank you.

Barev; Armenian for Hello

Medz Yeghern; "Great Evil Crime" (Armenian)

Last names connected to or associated with Karamardian family: Injejikian, Aslanian, Giragossian, Chalakian, Margosian, Karagozian, Karagosian, Titizian, M'gerditchian, Boghossian, Churukian, Sarkissian, Apelian, Terterian, Ashekian, Nazarian, Kakusian, Asarian, Hasessian, Ayanian, Berber

BIBLIOGRAPHY AND RECOMMENDED READING

Arlen, Michael J. *Passage to Ararat.* Farrar, Strauss and Giroux, 1975.

Balakian, Peter. *The Black Dog of Fate.* Basic Books, 1997.

Balakian, Peter. *The Burning Tigris: The Armenian Genocide and America's Response.* Harper Collins, 2003.

Bohjalian, Chris. *Sandcastle Girls.* Knopf Doubleday Publishing Group, 2013.

Edgarian, Carol. *Rise the Euphrates.* Random House, 1994.

Hovannisian, Richard G. *The Republic of Armenia, Volumes 1 – 4.* Univ. of California Press, 1971.

Hovannisian, Richard G. *Armenian People from Ancient to Modern Times Vols I and II.* Palgrave MacMillan US, 1997.

Kessab Educational Association. *Kessab and the Kessabtsis: Special edition commemorating 50th anniversary.* KEA of LA, Calif, USA, 2011.

Marcom, Micheline Aharonian. *Three Apples Fell From Heaven, A Novel.* Riverhead Books, a member of Penguin Putnam, Inc., 2001.

Mouradian, Khatchig. *Resistance Network: The Armenian Genocide and Humanitarianism in Ottoman Syria 1915-1918.* Michigan State University Press, 2021.

Morganthau, Henry. *Ambassador Morganthau's Story; A Personal Account of the Armenian Genocide.* Original publish date 1918. Reprinted with Edwin Mellen Press, 2022.

Pattie, Susan Paul. *The Armenian Legionnaires: Sacrifice and Betrayal in WWI.* I.B. Tauris, 2018.

Sanjian, Avedis. *Armenian Communities in Syria under Ottoman Dominion.* Harvard University Press, 1965.

Sarkissian, Hagop. *From Kessab to Watertown: A Modern Saga.* Ohan Press, 1966.

Werfel, Frantz. *The Forty Days of Musa Dagh.* Fischer Verlag, translate David R. Godine, 1933.

Online resources

100 Years of Reformed Presbyterian Missions in Syria: Part 1 of 2 retrieved from Gentlereformation.com

Various entries retrieved from Presbyterianmission.org

Author Unknown (2015, August, 12) The Dominican Republic and its Arab Assimilation. Retrieved from Abreu Report: Global Politics.

Unpublished

George Peter. *Karamardian Kapers - personal journal writings.*

Laura Peter Smith. Various letters, 1942-1947.

NOTE ON FICTION AND TRUTH

The ***Odar*** series is a work of fiction, though based on true events, true people, and mostly authentic attitude and personality. I seem to have exhausted (of my ability and to my knowledge) access to information through documented research. And I have incorporated most of what I gratefully received through first, second and third hand interviews. Yet, I fully expect additional detail to appear after publication of this work; perhaps via relatives as yet unknown to me, perhaps from less likely sources or from completely unexpected windfall. After many decades of searching and processing clues and details, nothing would surprise me.

For all the factual detail existing in *Odar,* I found it most feasible to fully share the story of Joe Peter and the settling of his several communities during historic times as a work of fiction, in order to best see the members of one family in all their human thought and action. Imagination served for certain details of action, plot and character development – gaps filled in, opinions, thoughts, and sentiments assigned. There is no way to share the material facts in my possession without some guesswork as to the heart at the center of them. I sincerely hope not to cause inconvenience to any living person via my method or for any error I may have inadvertently ascribed to real people through the telling.

I have not changed names in this story. In fact, I have taken the liberty to include real names and places gleaned from census records, passenger lists, naturalization applications, and other available documentation and assign them roles. I chose to insert real people into the lives of my ancestors where I deemed the association likely and logical, or heard mention of said persons in interviews or through family folklore. Since this telling is about real people and real places, I found little reason to fabricate in cases where names are available on record.

Finally, to quote author Yiyun Li (The New Yorker, Oct 30, 2023): "Some fiction is tamer than some life…"

I could not have expressed in a better way, the end result of the story I have laid out in these pages. Naturally, there is more than a little family drama that I have omitted. Family folklore or secrets unearthed by accident tend to exist within the fabric of most families. In this case, certain sensational details, of murder and mayhem, may well deserve their own storyline in a full volume, while detracting from this one. So yes, this work of fiction may be somewhat tamer than the complete unabridged life of Joseph Peter and/or the greater Karamardian family. But this is the story I have chosen to tell. I hope, and believe, it is enough. And that the reader has gained from the telling.

Most importantly, I dedicate this series to all of my family and to families everywhere, in all their glory and complication. And to the memory of all ancestors.

Denice Peter Karamardian

GRATITUDE RUNS DEEP

There are few words for the depth of my feelings for the primary angels of this project. First and foremost, my inspiration, my collaborator and connecting thread, a primary voice and soulmate in the journey – my late father, **George Peter,** who talked and wrote about his life and helped to access and interview first generation major characters in the book, his aunts. I dedicate every word to him, in absentia. I hope he is enjoying eternal space with the others, and the ancestors.

Sossi (Karamardian) Madzounian, my angel guide, facilitated my search and discovery with hospitality beyond belief, directed me far and wide, introduced me to the Kessab community in L.A. and continually inspires me, along with her entire family. *Ilene Karagozian Hill,* my inaugural host/guide who helped me launch discovery with graciousness, care and interest. *Lisa Bennett*, my first editor, helped shape a story line from dense quantity of material into a first draft with patience and mind blowing guidance and wisdom.

The storytellers were crucial blessings in my life to the endeavor. As witnesses, they evolved into the major character and storytellers of Odar. Their words reached out, some from final days on a sofa, others from the great beyond, to shape the world and challenges they had known and overcome: **Marta Karamardian Karagozian, Alice Karamardian Margosian, Serop Karamardian, Louisa Guzelian Karamardian,**

ChiChi (Florence) Karagosian, and Dr. Vahan Churukian. (The females listed here spoke in absentia.) Their stories were augmented (and some narrated) by **Mary Boghossian Karamardian, Armine Boghossian Thomson, Seta Der Terossian Karamardian Soma, Stepan Karamardian, and Madame Rosa Karamardian**. Profound witnessing over many decades, which shaped much of the narration for the story of Odar, came from closer to home: **John Peter, Susie Peter Bakerjian, and Laura Peter Smith** (my father's siblings).

All of the above have deceased since my interviews with them. So too, have some of the second generation witnesses who provided in depth information and enhanced experience: **Gabriel Injejikian, Neva Karamardian, Harry Karagosian, Colleen Karagozian; Cut, Barbara** and **Lorraine Abraham.** I am so very grateful for the sharing of their memories of old world childhoods from *Garbis Karamardian, Anoush Karamardian Tohikian, and Kerop Kazarian.* And then of course, more miraculously appearing relatives with revelations: *Khatchig Titizian, Laurie Cunnington and the Simon sisters.*

There was much additional help from ....*Gary Lind-Sinanian* - curator, Armenian Library and Museum of America, Watertown, MA.; *Makda Watherspoon* of Cornell Arabic Department for document translations; *Kessab Educational Center*, Los Angeles, CA; *Carol Kammen*, historian, for an Ithaca initiation to research; *Lansing Historical Society and Salt Point Park exhibit*; *Peter Balakian*, author, for trailblazing guidance, research, and inspiration; my French translators in Paris, France *Nicholas Karamardian, Karim Bachiri, and Nadea; Jana Hextor*, medium; the *Cornell Armenian Student Association*, language classes and social support.

A very special shout out to *Steven Manley* for graphic support, *Jeffrey Smith*, for technical design (map) and technical support (photos), and once again to the very talented Sossi Madzounian for cover art (photographic for all jacket covers).

I'm grateful for additional support from cousins: *Dan and John Karagozian, Larry Bakerjian, Lark Karamardian, Alice Karamardian Vartabedian, Elo Tohikian*, and *Liza Karamardian Carter*. Also *Leslie Daniels*, author, for helpful advice and a first look at book content, *Alison Wearing*, (Stratford, Canada) memoire instructor, and my very patient friend and early copy editor, *Donna Ramer*.

Thank you to more **editors:** *Kate Allyson, Brian Dooley, Ashley Swanson*. **Last, but never least**, **early readers and cheerleaders**.....*Mary Helen Myrdek, Paula Peter, Vally Kovary, Maureen Moore, Vicky Hutchinson, Michael J. Peter, Daniel Terino, Donna Ramer*, and *Patrice DiLorenzo*.

Note: names in bold represent deceased participants

ABOUT THE AUTHOR

Photo by T.C. Peter 2022

Denice Peter Karamardian owns and operates a regional publication for Finger Lakes wine visitors and is at work on several books. She is retired from a rich tapestry of overlapping careers that spanned over forty plus years and included instructing voice, host/producer of radio concert broadcast series, fifty years of music and theater performance, columnist and reviewer. She currently lives in her hometown of Ithaca, New York (where she operated a bed and breakfast for two decades) near/with her family.

Made in the USA
Columbia, SC
27 July 2024

de574383-263f-4d65-9880-a902ea84c6f9R03